Letts EXPLORE

Hamlet

WILLIAM SHAKESPEARE

D0784525

Guide written by
Stewart Martin

A Letts Literature Guide

Every effort has been made to trace copyright holders and to obtain their permission for the use of copyright material. The author and publishers will gladly receive information enabling them to rectify any reference or credit in subsequent editions.

First published 1995
Reprinted 1996

Letts Educational
Aldine House
Aldine Place
London W12 8AW
0181 740 2266

Text © Stewart Martin 1995

Typeset by Jordan Publishing Design

Text Design Jonathan Barnard

Cover and text illustrations Hugh Marshall

Graphic illustration Hugh Marshall

Design © BPP (Letts Educational) Ltd

British Library Cataloguing in Publication Data
A CIP record for this book is available from the British Library

ISBN 1 85758 268 3

Printed and bound in Great Britain by
Ashford Colour Press Ltd, Gosport, Hants

Letts Educational is the trading name of BPP (Letts Educational) Ltd

Contents

Plot synopsis

The story takes place in ancient Denmark, although the geographical setting – as with many of Shakespeare's plays – is not critical and the play abounds with references to contemporary (Elizabethan) England. The action opens with sentries witnessing the appearance of the Ghost of the late king one night on the castle wall in Elsinore. The present king is Claudius, brother of the late king. Claudius has married his dead brother's wife, with whom he has had an incestuous relationship. We learn from Claudius about the threat of an invasion from Norway and his plans to prevent it.

Hamlet, the son of the late king, is unhappy about his mother's marriage to Claudius and is still mourning his father's death. Hamlet has become withdrawn of late and wishes to return to his studies at university in Wittenberg, but agrees to stay when it becomes clear that his mother and Claudius want him to remain at Elsinore. When Hamlet learns of the earlier appearance of his father's ghost he is anxious to see it for himself and, when he does so, learns from it that his father was murdered by Claudius. The Ghost makes Hamlet promise to avenge the murder.

Polonius, an important courtier, decides that Hamlet's recent separation from the affections of his daughter, Ophelia, has made him mad and tells this to Claudius. Polonius and Claudius secretly observe a meeting between Hamlet and Ophelia at which Hamlet speaks wildly. Claudius recruits Rosencrantz and Guildenstern, two of Hamlet's fellow students, to spy on Hamlet.

A group of travelling actors present a play to the court. Hamlet has arranged for the play to depict a re-enactment of his father's murder and Claudius' reaction on seeing this convinces Hamlet of his guilt. Later in a soliloquy, Claudius confesses his guilt and prays for forgiveness. Hamlet sees Claudius at prayer and considers killing him on the spot but decides to wait until he catches him doing something wicked, so that his soul will then go to hell.

The ghost of Hamlet's father appears again as Hamlet criticises his mother for her behaviour. Hamlet mistakes the presence of Polonius, hiding behind a curtain, for Claudius and kills him. The Ghost urges Hamlet to pity his mother, the Queen, and reminds him of his promise to avenge the murder. Later the Queen tells Claudius about Polonius' death. The King sends Hamlet with Rosencrantz and Guildenstern to England – supposedly for

Hamlet's safety – but plans to have him murdered there.

Ophelia becomes insane and rambles wildly. Laertes arrives at the castle demanding revenge for the death of his father Polonius. On receiving a letter from Hamlet, thereby proving that his plan to have Hamlet murdered in England has failed, Claudius plots with Laertes to ensure the death of Hamlet by means of a fencing match in which an unblunted sword with a poisoned blade will be used, together with poisoned wine.

At the burial of Ophelia, after her suicide by drowning, Hamlet and Laertes fight. During the pre-arranged fencing match, the Queen accidentally drinks the poisoned wine and both Hamlet and Laertes are wounded with the poisoned sword. The King's plot is revealed by the dying Laertes. Hamlet wounds the King with the poisoned sword then forces him to drink the poisoned wine. The King and Queen die, along with Laertes and Hamlet.

Different editions of a Shakespeare play are usually very similar, although they may show occasional variation in spelling, punctuation and the arrangement of the lines. You may even come across differences in act or scene divisions but this should produce no difficulties for you in identifying the particular point or section being commented on in this Guide. The quotations and comments in this Guide are referenced to the Arden edition of the play.

WHO INFLUENCED THE BARD?

Candidates for Shakespeare's sources for *Hamlet* are many and varied.
Consult the notes on pp8–9 for more information on some of the
main probabilities, but be aware that relatively little consensus exists
as to the extent to which Shakespeare may have used each of them.

Roman times 9thC

12thC Histoires Tragiques

Antonio's Revenge – Marston

1592 Pierce Penniles

1586 Treatise

1623

Belleforest

1588 The Ur-Hamlet

His Supplication to the Devil, Thomas Nashe

of Melancholy, Timothy Bright

1599–1601 The Tragical History of Hamlet, Prince of Denmark, Shakespeare

1603 Quarto 1 (Q1)   1604 Quarto 2 (Q2)

The First Folio edition (F)

Traggedia Der Bestrafte Brudermord (Fraticide Punished)

Who influenced the Bard?

Shakespeare's use of his sources for the play remains uncertain, but much earlier and contemporary material seems likely to have been known to him. Although anything which Shakespeare knew of could have – and probably did – contribute to *Hamlet*, we have no way of knowing which if any of the sources below he may have consulted.

In legends dating from Roman times we find mention of an avenging son who drove Rome's enemies from the capital city and references of this nature also appear in the ninth-century Icelandic legends about a character called Amleth. In addition to the works mentioned below, and to his usual historical sources in Plutarch's *Lives* and Virgil's *Aeneid*, there are many other contemporary works and events which Shakespeare may have been influenced by. For example, in October 1538 news was circulating throughout Europe of the murder of the Duke of Urbino – a famous military and political figure of the time – rumoured to have been killed by poison being put into his ears. The Duke's barber surgeon was tortured and confessed to the deed, claiming he was acting under the orders of Luigi Gonzaga, a kinsman of the Duchess, although Gonzaga's guilt was never proved.

Perhaps the first written account which we could call a 'source' for *Hamlet* is the twelfth-century *Historiae Danicae* by Saxo Grammaticus, first published in Latin in 1514. This story is the earliest known written account of the character – Amleth – whom we now know as Hamlet. Amleth's mother Gerutha (Shakespeare's Gertrude) has married Fengo, her husband's brother. The plot has many similarities to Shakespeare's: fratricide, an incestuous marriage, a pretended madness, a long delayed revenge, a man who spies on the hero in his mother's chambers, courtiers who escort him to England to be murdered, and a final vengeance achieved through a change of swords. There are also many echoes of dialogue in important scenes.

In 1570 the seventh volume of Belleforest's *Histoires Tragiques* brought Saxo's story to the Elizabethans and is widely seen as a main source for Shakespeare. Belleforest embellished the tale and introduced a pronounced moralising tone, apologising to his audience for what they might see as the more uncivilised parts of the story and the ungracious behaviour of some characters. Belleforest introduces the notion, absent in Saxo, that Hamlet's mother was seduced by her husband's brother *before* the murder. There is also some anticipation of Shakespeare's development of the ghost. Whilst there are some echoes in Shakespeare of the behaviour of characters in Belleforest, there are no real echoes in the language apart from the occasional word. Whether Belleforest came to Shakespeare directly or via a source which has been called the 'Ur-Hamlet' is unknown.

Some writers have supposed that the Ur-Hamlet was written by Thomas Kyd around 1588, although many others have assumed he used the Ur-Hamlet as the basis for his play, *The Spanish Tragedy* (1588–89), which some see as an influence on *Hamlet*. The Ur-Hamlet is seen by many as Shakespeare's chief source for his play. There are no copies of the text of Ur-Hamlet and, though a popular play at the time, it seems never to have been printed, although scholars have made numerous attempts to reconstruct it from contemporary accounts. A special feature of the Ur-Hamlet was the ghost, which many scholars think Shakespeare used and adapted.

Antonio's Revenge, by Marston, is believed by some critics to be later than *Hamlet*, whilst others believe it to be earlier. It contains many echoes of plot, incident, setting and language to *Hamlet* and scholars disagree as to which owes a debt to the other. Possibly both plays owe their common likeness to the Ur-Hamlet.

Thomas Nashe wrote *Pierce Penniless His Supplication to the Devil*, in 1592 and this popular pamphlet, especially notable for its depiction of the character of the Danish court and its supposed habitual drunkenness, seems to have been a clear influence on Shakespeare.

In 1586 the *Treatise of Melancholy*, by Timothy Bright, appeared and although scholars think it unlikely that Shakespeare used Bright, his work is a good example of the kind of authoritative work common at the time on the 'Elizabethan Malady' of melancholy.

Shakespeare's own work, *The Tragical History of Hamlet, Prince of Denmark*, was most probably written in late 1599 or early 1600 – possibly in 1601. The varying dates depend on whether we accept (as some critics do) that *Hamlet* was written all of a piece or, as others argue, was amended after 1599–1600 to include the references to the rival acting companies which dominated the theatrical life of London in 1601. The text of the play was first published in 1603. In 1603 Quarto 1 (Q1) appeared. Known as the bad quarto, Q1 is a version of the play thought to be pieced together from actors' memories. In 1604 Quarto 2 (Q2) appeared and is a good copy, thought to be reproduced from Shakespeare's own manuscript, but corrected occasionally against Q1 where this was clearer. Unfortunately Q2 has some scenes cut out: for example, Hamlet's thoughts about Denmark being like a prison (this was possibly because the new King James I had a Danish wife). Other omissions include the references to the rival acting companies. Quarto 2 was subsequently reprinted as Quartos 3, 4 and 5.

The First Folio edition (F) of the play was printed in 1623 and was based on Q2, with corrections and added stage directions, but incorporated other errors, omissions and mis-copyings. However, F includes the scenes omitted from Q2. Modern editions of the play usually cross-reference Q2 and F.

Traggedia Der Bestrafte Brudermord (Fratricide Punished) is a work which some critics have argued is descended from the Ur-Hamlet. Others see it as a poor, rough version of Shakespeare's *Hamlet*, which was taken to Germany and much corrupted, probably long before it appeared in print in England.

Hamlet

Hamlet

The character of Hamlet is subtle and complex, even by the standards of Shakespeare, and has been the focus of a copious and growing commentary, much of it contradictory. In seeking to clarify what we understand and feel about the play, it is important to recognise what we have before us. Shakespeare often concerned himself with the flawed nature of humanity and one of the play's dominant features is the way Hamlet comes to accept that humanity contains both good and evil. He accepts that even Claudius has a conscience which the players may 'catch' but finds it hard to come to terms with his mother's guilt and is persuaded that every woman is a 'breeder of sinners'. Hamlet's love for his mother and for Ophelia is corrupted by this realisation and his obsessive revulsion of sex and love leads him to savage them both and to criticise his own failings and those of humankind.

However, the presentation on stage of Hamlet's troubled mind is not a deliberate anticipation of some of the psychologically realistic characters of modern drama. It is instead a dramatic construction for presenting the audience with a philosophical attitude. Naturalistic interpretations of the play reject this view, and argue that Hamlet has a problem in that he thinks too much and acts too little. Most debate on this seems to revolve around arguments about why Hamlet delays in carrying out the Ghost's order to avenge his father's murder. Although it is interesting – and can be revealing – to see Hamlet as a character in the sense of being a real personality, it can also produce confusing problems. No particular interpretation of a play is ever 'right' in the sense that others are 'wrong', and providing a viewpoint can be supported by the text it is legitimate. *Hamlet* is a masterpiece written by an artist at the height of his powers and which supports many different interpretations; it is important to recognise this when forming your own view of things. How you tend to regard the play – as a naturalistic portrayal of individuals or more as a dramatic device – will shape your thinking. Clarity about where your own general standpoint is will help you avoid some difficulties as you study the play, but try to remain open to the insights offered by other views. That is what drama is all about.

Hamlet's abiding preoccupation with appearance and reality ranges across the flaws and goodness in humankind, the possibility of an afterlife and the seductive appeal of suicide. We first meet Hamlet as he grieves for his dead father, a man of nobility and a great king. Hamlet's emotional trauma has been increased by his mother's hasty and incestuous marriage to his father's brother, Claudius. When his father's ghost reveals that Claudius is his murderer, Hamlet is tortured by the notion that his mother could wed – and bed – such an evil creature. Desolate and tortured, Hamlet briefly contemplates suicide but rejects it and instead is preoccupied by his mother's sexual betrayal. Hamlet's feelings of disgust, anger, grief and betrayal transfer to Ophelia and this leads him to deny his love for her. Hamlet is thereby able to deny and punish his mother's sexuality by displacing her guilt onto Ophelia. He is able to reject love, sex, marriage and life in the face of the Ghost's injunction to hold no evil thought against his mother. The extent to which Hamlet really becomes mad – or only seems so – has always vexed critics and it is hard not to sympathise with Oscar Wilde's oft quoted witticism, 'Are the critics mad or only pretending to be so?'

Commentators also disagree on the extent to which Hamlet delays in avenging his father's murder, if at all, and whether or not he really suspected that Claudius, and not Polonius, was hiding behind the arras in his mother's room. Some feel that Hamlet's character descends into evil in Act 3, during which Ophelia takes her own life and Hamlet is exiled to England. Others argue that he is still attempting to reconcile himself to his own fate. By Act 5 a more mature Hamlet emerges, one who can meditate upon life's frailties without bitterness or fear. Hamlet's memories of Yorick are fond, and although his passion is aroused at the graveside of Ophelia when he fights with Laertes, he eventually becomes subdued enough to withdraw. Hamlet has shed what seems to have been the paralysing grief of Act 1 and now accepts his destiny and has become reconciled to the flawed nature of humankind and its place in the universal order of creation. He also accepts his own human failings and that he must prepare for his own death, a death which will release him in salvation from the burden which the Ghost placed upon him.

Part of the richness and ambiguity of Hamlet's character is to do with how he is presented to us. In only seven scenes in the play — several of them very brief — is Hamlet not centre-stage, and in many of those seven he is the main topic of conversation. Hamlet is presented to us as a kaleidoscope of different images: through his own eyes in his soliloquies; through the fearful eyes of Claudius; from the viewpoint of his friend Horatio and that of the interfering busybody Polonius; and as perceived by his doting mother Gertrude and his rejected lover Ophelia.

Claudius

Claudius

Claudius I was a Roman emperor (10 B.C. to 54 A.D.) who the Elizabethans regarded as the epitome of an evil ruler. He entered into an incestuous marriage with his niece, Agrippa, who later poisoned him and was then herself murdered by her son Nero. Hamlet alludes to this in Act 3, scene 2. The crime of Claudius permeates the play's world and is the manifestation of evil that is in it. He is not, however, the out and out villain which Hamlet describes and the audience need to assess carefully whether they agree with Hamlet or see any remorse in the behaviour of Claudius.

The context in which Claudius exists as a character is that set by Hamlet's dead father, who is described in idealised terms and Claudius, as his murderer, is contrasted with this ideal throughout the play. Claudius has also wed Gertrude, Hamlet's mother, and he epitomises the rottenness that Hamlet sees in Denmark. Claudius is often associated with the excessive drinking for which the Danes were noted by Shakespeare's audience and it is a neat irony that it is this symbol of his dissolute, intemperate and wicked nature which poisons him at the end of the play. Although most commentators feel that Claudius is abundantly wicked this view is not universal. Shakespeare typically gives us scope to see Claudius as having several worthy features, being quick-witted, intelligent, often reasonable and a competent and decisive king. We also know him to have some feelings of conscience about murdering Hamlet's father, as shown in his soliloquy in Act 3, scene 3. Most critics view Claudius as wicked, however, drawing attention to his deliberate scheming to have Hamlet murdered in England. Equally, and parallel to his own deed, Claudius contrives to have Hamlet's death occur via a betrayal at the hands of his friends. Claudius also conspires with Laertes to arrange the death of Hamlet, again by devious means. When Laertes eventually confesses the plot to Hamlet and asks forgiveness the focus of guilt returns again exclusively to Claudius.

Claudius shows himself to be a bold plotter and skilled opportunist, in contrast to Hamlet who finds action difficult. He uses the murder of Polonius – and skilfully exploits the anger of Laertes – as devices by which he tries to destroy Hamlet. But it is the actions of Claudius which finally are his undoing, not the stratagems of Hamlet. Although Hamlet eventually avenges his father's murder, this is achieved by his virtuous acceptance of his destiny and by the failure of the plotting of Claudius. Elizabethan belief would hold that because Claudius attempted immorally to subvert the natural world-order he had to be punished.

The dramatic relationship between Hamlet and Claudius is the axis about which the action of the play turns and the tension between them is the key to understanding the play. The character of Hamlet is more developed and engages with the audience more directly through his soliloquies and his relationships with other characters. On the other hand, Claudius initiates more of the action, which generates a dramatic balance between his character and that of Hamlet, but he is drawn less sympathetically – not least because of his evil actions.

Gertrude

Gertrude

Although Queen Gertrude has married her husband's brother with such haste that it has troubled her son Hamlet, we have no evidence that she is aware that Claudius has gained the throne by murder. We do know from the Ghost that Gertrude had an adulterous relationship with Claudius before he became king, but that the Ghost attributes Gertrude's evil to her weakness and blames Claudius for exploiting it. The audience has to decide whether they feel it believable that a woman who really loved her son as much as Gertrude declared she loved Hamlet could dishonour his father by an incestuous and over-hasty marriage. Like that of Claudius, the character of Gertrude remains relatively undeveloped. She exists as a character more in relationship to other characters in the play than as a rounded figure in her own right. At first we see her as supporting Claudius in calling for Hamlet to shed his excessive grief. Later this turns to a sharper concern for her son's welfare when she rejects the assumption by Polonius that unrequited love has turned him mad. We hear most from Gertrude when, in a beautiful and touching speech, she describes Ophelia's death, but even then she is a bystander to the play's main action. She dies, like her earlier husband, by poison at the hand of Claudius.

Ophelia

Ophelia

Ophelia is depicted as beautiful, pure and sexually innocent (but not naive) and therefore as a contrast to Gertrude. No character in the play ever has anything evil to say about Ophelia and of all the main characters she is the only one who is without guilt, deviousness or evil. In her madness, which stems from her father's death and Hamlet's rejection of her, we see her preoccupation with her father Polonius and her lover Hamlet, and her pathetic fantasies about her now blighted future. Ophelia lacks the strength and maturity to survive her father's murder or Hamlet's rejection of her and this heightens the sadness surrounding the madness and death of this affectionate and gentle character.

However, she is not merely a passive victim and we see several examples of her wit and character in her exchanges with Hamlet and her brother Laertes. That she loved Hamlet profoundly is never in serious doubt and even Hamlet's rejection of her is due more to the displacement of his disgust with his mother's behaviour than a failure within their own relationship itself. By the time we first see Ophelia and Hamlet together the play is almost half done and Hamlet is rejecting her, whether in some measure in feigned madness or in suspicion that she is a pawn for Polonius and Claudius we do not know. By the time we reach scene 5 in Act 4 Polonius has been murdered by Hamlet and she is genuinely mad, in contrast to Hamlet's 'disposition' to be mad. By suggesting that Hamlet is merely trifling with her and that he is in any case not free to marry, Laertes and Polonius effectively poison the relationship. The character of Ophelia is often used in the play to throw light upon Hamlet's predicament and, like other characters in the play, she finds herself caught between 'the pass and fell incensed points/Of mighty opposites' and is destroyed in the process.

Polonius

Polonius

Polonius is in some ways an example of the rottenness in Denmark, or perhaps a reaction to it, as he is a scheming and dishonest character who loves espionage and sees intrigue everywhere. He seems unable to leave well alone and, like his master Claudius, is the agent of his own undoing. As the father of Laertes and Ophelia, Polonius is an important connection between many of the play's other characters and it is his killing by Hamlet which precipitates the final action of the play. His advice to his son 'to thine own self be true' is typical of his hypocritical attitude, for he trusts no one. He spies on his own son, uses his own daughter as part of his intrigue, spies on Ophelia and Hamlet himself and his immediate thought on being in Gertrude's chamber when Hamlet arrives is to see this as yet another opportunity for deviousness. Yet, it is clear that Polonius cares for his children and is dearly loved in return by them, and therefore his killing by Hamlet should not be seen simply as an impetuous act devoid of deliberate evil.

The Fool

The Fool

The Fool – or Clown – as a character in his own right, does not appear in *Hamlet*. Instead we see the Fool as an aspect of several other characters. Polonius, for example, behaves in a very comic but significant and revealing way on a number of occasions. As someone who asserts that 'brevity is the soul of wit' he is wonderfully long-winded and circuitous in arriving at his point. When Gertrude challenges him to produce 'more matter with less art', he declares with unwitting irony that he uses 'no art at all', and in the exchanges with Hamlet he is ragged mercilessly almost every time they meet, especially in Act 2 scene 2 and in Act 3 scene 3. Sometimes Hamlet himself plays the Fool, both in his 'antic disposition', and sometimes in his exchanges with Ophelia. He also makes a fool not only of Polonius but also of his two school fellows. Other characters who can be seen to carry the Fool's part in some measure are Rosencrantz and Guildenstern, Osric and the grave-digger, who has a very matter-of-fact approach to death.

Laertes

As the stock character of the 'avenging brother' Laertes behaves, as we might expect, with traditional recklessness and ruthlessness. He serves as a warning against the dangers of reckless passion, for he is easily moulded by the cunning Claudius. In this regard he serves as a contrast to Horatio, who considers carefully before acting, whilst Laertes bursts into situations and loses his temper. Unlike Hamlet, Laertes is granted permission to return to his studies abroad, but before he goes he gives advice to Ophelia to beware of Hamlet. Ironically, he describes Hamlet in terms better suited to his own character and his clumsy advice is comically echoed by his father, Polonius, who gives his son some equally heavy-handed guidance.

However, at the end of the play we see Laertes generously confess his wicked deeds against Hamlet, repent and gain forgiveness. In this noble gesture he is marked off from Claudius, who is left holding all the blame for the tragedy. Laertes, like Hamlet, successfully seeks revenge for his father's murder, dies in doing so and gains forgiveness from his own killer. Unlike Hamlet, Laertes is immature and shallow, easily manipulated and quick to adopt and embellish any underhanded methods he can in order to achieve his ends.

Horatio

Horatio is Hamlet's trustworthy and courageous friend. He is also a realistic and practical person who is at first very sceptical about the Ghost's existence. He remains loyal to Hamlet throughout the play and helps him with 'The Mousetrap' in catching Claudius. His cool and sincere response to situations marks him as a man of caution. As Hamlet's confidante he also provides an audience for his friend. At the end it is only because Hamlet persuades him otherwise that he does not die with his friend, agreeing instead to follow Hamlet's orders to 'draw thy breath in pain to tell my story.'

Rosencrantz and Guildenstern

These two school friends of Hamlet find his conversation impossible to follow and conclude, like Polonius, that he is mad. This reinforces our sense of Hamlet's isolation from other characters. They become part of the plotting of Claudius and pay dearly for it when Hamlet sends them to their death in his place. Their passing is not mourned by Hamlet, who says that they were willing servants of the King, although we have no direct evidence that they knew of the King's plans or that they are evil men. Rosencrantz and Guildenstern are treated as the two halves of one character and represent the kind of person who will do anything to serve those currently in power in return for advancement. They are servile in their willingness to do anything which the King commands and are further examples of the rottenness which is in Denmark, in contrast to the loyal Horatio.

The Grave-digger

The grave-digger and his companion ('another') are two stock 'rustic clown' characters and, like the 'mad' scene with Ophelia, are part of a theatrical tradition which was well understood by the audiences in Shakespeare's time. The interlude with the grave-digger is not intended to develop the plot of the play, but is instead a device to heighten the coming tension by means of dramatic contrast – a lightening of the tone before the rapidly approaching climax to the action. Yet Shakespeare makes more of the interlude than this; the grave-digger acts almost as a chorus on the main action, reflecting on the nature of reality and appearance and on what words say as opposed to what they mean; and commenting on the world of Denmark and the mortality of humankind. By giving the grave-digger this role, Shakespeare is also able to suggest to the audience that Hamlet's previous preoccupation with mortality, death and suicide should now be seen not as a morbid wallowing in his own emotions, but as a realistic acceptance that death and decay are a natural part of human existence.

Osric

Osric is a foppish and affected courtier who, like Polonius (of whom he is a parody), is exposed to the gibes of Hamlet. As with Polonius, Hamlet shows how easily the obsequious and mannered behaviour of the Danish court can be used to make courtiers agree with completely contradictory comments and thereby ridicule themselves. Osric is more concerned with expression than content, and speaks 'more art with less matter' to misquote Gertrude. Osric's manner contrasts with Hamlet's determination to do what must be done; whilst Hamlet is in deadly earnest, Osric sees his umpiring of the duel as just another amusing interlude, a routine part of courtly life.

■ Themes and images in *Hamlet*

Appearance and Reality

Appearance and Reality

The play reflects an abiding interest of Shakespeare's age, as well as of the playwright himself, in the difference between the world as it appears to be and as it really is. This appears in many aspects of *Hamlet*; the grave-digger debates the nature of suicide and reflects on human mortality, and his witty exchanges with his partner reflect the underlying seriousness with which the play examines what is and what appears to be. The first lines of the play, where sentinels seek the true identity of others in the darkness, reflect the play's abiding concern with distinguishing reality and safety from deception, danger and madness. The Ghost is an important aspect of these reflections.

There is much preoccupation with all kinds of 'acting' in the play and only the most obvious example is the play-within-the-play, when the Player-King's passion gives Hamlet cause to ponder his own reasons for killing the King. Hamlet's 'antic disposition' is both an examination of the nature of what it is to be mad or sane and what it is to play a part – contrasted with Ophelia's real madness – and a mask from behind which he may duel with other characters. As with all the characters in the play who seem to wear, or be trapped behind, a mask this encourages the audience to wonder how sure each character is of their own nature. Claudius 'smiles and smiles' but seems a villain in spite of his flash of conscience, Hamlet 'knowest not seems' but at times behaves as though he does not know who he is himself. Everywhere we find characters spying, sending false messages, twisting their words, appearing to be one thing to each other whilst in reality being another. Intrigue is used by characters in their attempts to uncover the real motives of others and characters are used as players in deadly games of which they themselves are often unaware – Ophelia, the players, Rosencrantz and Guildenstern and Osric are all used in this way. Even objects are not what they seem: a deceiving letter is sent by Claudius with Hamlet to England, the cup of wine and the fencing swords are also, like the play which Hamlet organises, not what they appear to be.

Order and Disorder

Order and Disorder

The conflict between order and disorder is a central theme of the play which appears right at the start and is present throughout. The Elizabethan's philosophical notions about the world and the importance in it of divine order appear frequently in the imagery and action: where a rightful and noble king is murdered by a brother driven by greed for power and the sexual lust found between the 'incestuous sheets' of the queen's bed; where a tormented spirit cannot attain grace but is condemned to torture in purgatory until released by revenge; where political intrigue and drunken revelry has rotted the fabric of good government in the state; where honest dealing between people has been replaced by suspicion and plotting; and where at every turn surface appearances conceal a destructive disorder underneath.

The play begins and ends in settings which emphasise the emptiness of death and its shadow falls across every scene in the play; Hamlet himself bears its stamp, carrying his despair from the start through the action and scenes of increasing destruction to the dead march which concludes the final act. The imagery, as often in Shakespeare, links the action, connecting together in complex and subtle ways ideas about decay, disease and corruption with the desecration of the holy state of marriage, the diseases of the physical body, the emotional and mental faculties of characters and the rottenness of the political fabric of the state – all of which, as well as the time itself, are dislocated and 'out of joint'. Hamlet speaks of his mother's incest in terms of 'the rank sweat of an enseamed bed, stew'd in corruption' (Act 3, scene 4), echoing the Ghost's condemnation of the 'shameful lust' which will 'sate itself in a celestial bed and prey on garbage' (Act 1, scene 5). Claudius is described by the Ghost as a thing unclean, something which must be cast out. Hamlet knows that the Ghost itself may be a 'goblin damned' or an image of the Devil. The world itself is for Hamlet 'an unweeded garden', the sky 'a foul and pestilent congregation of vapours', and man himself nothing but a 'quintessence of dust'. The supposed descent of Hamlet into madness, and Ophelia's genuine madness, are more intensely personal but lesser echoes of the larger destruction which has been wrought around them by the murder of Hamlet's father and the usurping of the throne.

Revenge

Revenge

During Elizabethan times there were mixed views about revenge. Traditionally revenge had been seen as unmistakably correct, a manner of dispensing justice, and it is this role which Laertes adopts in the play. Other views held that revenge was a sin. Both perspectives are applied within *Hamlet*, as are the countervailing arguments against each. The essential supposition behind the play, and without which it will not work, is that a son should avenge the murder of his father. Hamlet himself seems to accept this as a basis from which he *ought* to act, but his equivocation about the good or evil nature of the Ghost highlights the unease of his age about the danger of succumbing to evil whilst being driven by pure motives, even ones as pure as filial love and honour. By its own admission the Ghost comes not from heaven, nor from hell, but from the purgatory of eternal suffering to which it is condemned because Hamlet's father died in a state of sin, with no time to ask forgiveness for all his sins and therefore, as the Ghost says, 'with all my imperfections on my head'. The spur to Hamlet's action is the relief of the Ghost from the fires which burn away the 'foul crimes' committed whilst it was alive. This tension between the dual nature of humankind and the mingling of thought and action, evil and good, runs throughout the play.

Sex, Love and Marriage

Sex, Love and Marriage

Several characters in the play are connected by sexual relationships, love, or marriage. Hamlet becomes preoccupied with what he sees as his mother's sexual betrayal of her husband. Gertrude's incestuous marriage to Claudius, following her adultery with him, disgusts her son who finds it hard to understand how she can have lusted

21

after a man who is, in all respects, his father's inferior. Hamlet's disgust and disillusionment with women transfer to Ophelia and this blights their past love. Ophelia's torment derives from loving her father as well as his murderer and mirrors the situation of Gertrude. This leads to Ophelia's suicide and to the deaths of Claudius, Gertrude and Hamlet, punishing them all. Just as Gertrude's desire has, believes Hamlet, blinded her to reality so the Ghost is concerned that Hamlet's disgust with sexuality may blind him to his mother's redeeming features. Hamlet feels love and affection for many other characters, from his own father to his friend Horatio and Yorick, his play-mate of old. But with the exception of Horatio, and his friendliness towards the players, all Hamlet's affections end up being directed into the past, to times before his mother's 'o'erhasty marriage' and all the rottenness which seems to him to have flowed from it.

The parental affection of Polonius towards his children seems to have been corrupted by mistrust and plotting, to the point where he seems to regard his daughter as some kind of farmyard animal to be 'loosed' to Hamlet as part of a ploy to trap him into revealing something which Polonius can turn against him. Equally, Polonius sends spies to watch his own son, although it is also possible to see this behaviour as that of an over-anxious but genuinely loving parent. The character of Laertes, as the son of Polonius, behaves in the play as the traditional revenger who is motivated by love for his father's memory and, like Hamlet, dies in that cause.

■ Text commentary

Act 1 Scene 1

Barnardo and Francisco are watchers upon Elsinore's castle walls. They are joined by Marcellus and Horatio. The group are visited twice by a ghost which resembles the dead king. It refuses to speak to them when challenged, then seems as though it might, but when the cock crows it vanishes. They decide that they will tell Hamlet, the king's son, because they are sure that the ghost will speak to him.

Who's there?

Appearance and Reality

The first words of the play introduce us to the questioning of appearance and reality with which much of the action concerns itself. This first scene also sets an eerie tone which will catch the attention of the audience. Notice how it is some considerable time before the audience learn anything about why the Ghost has appeared and how this deliberate device cleverly builds the tension.

'Tis now struck twelve. Get thee to bed, Francisco

The imagery of sickness and disease which runs through the play is introduced when Barnardo comes to relieve the watch at midnight and Francisco complains of being 'sick at heart'. Notice also how the notion of things in Denmark being dislocated and that 'the time is out of joint' is subtly

Order and Disorder

introduced by the way it is Barnardo who challenges Francisco (who is the sentry on watch) and not the other way around.

Stay, speak, speak, I charge thee speak

Horatio has been invited along because, as a scholar and the friend of Hamlet, he may be able to explain why the Ghost keeps appearing. But the spirit will not speak to him and he muses that its appearance forebodes some 'strange eruption' in the state. About 20 lines further on, Marcellus asks why there is such preparation for war in the land. Horatio repeats the rumours he has heard, that young Fortinbras has gathered up an invasion force. This background is important because it introduces the important notion of a son avenging his father's death – in this case the death of old Fortinbras of Norway at the hand of the old King Hamlet of Denmark.

But look, the morn in russet mantle clad
Walks o'er the dew of yon high eastward hill

The Ghost leaves as the cock crows and Horatio and the others agree to tell Hamlet of events. Horatio is throughout a calmer, more objective observer of events than Hamlet, with whom he is identified as his close and trusted friend and with whom he forms a good dramatic contrast and balance. Hamlet's meeting with his dead father's ghost, which will speak to no one but him, sets the action of the play in motion.

Hamlet

It is some considerable time into the play before we meet Hamlet, and longer still before the audience engage with him directly through his first soliloquy. The early sections of the play serve therefore to set the scene for Hamlet's entry, but also serve to emphasise the way he is set apart from other characters.

Act 1 Scene 2

We meet the new king, Claudius, and hear of his marriage to his brother's wife Gertrude. Claudius has sent a message with Voltemand and Cornelius to the king of Norway to ask his help in calming the warlike ambitions of his nephew, Fortinbras, who is claiming some of Denmark's land. Claudius and Gertrude want the still grieving Hamlet to stay in Denmark, not go back to university in Wittenberg, although Polonius' son, Laertes, is given leave to go back to his studies in France. Hamlet agrees to stay and, when alone on stage, reflects sadly upon his mother's hurried and incestuous marriage to Claudius, following her husband's death. Horatio, Marcellus and Barnardo arrive and tell Hamlet about the ghost they have seen. Hamlet says he will go up on the castle walls that night to see the ghost himself and the others agree to keep the Ghost a secret.

And now, Laertes, what's the news with you?

The two sons Laertes and Hamlet parallel each other. Their identical requests to return abroad are answered differently by Claudius, heralding their differing roles in the forthcoming action. Claudius' mention of his debt to Polonius is intriguing. Polonius is sometimes depicted as nothing more than a talkative old fool, but you should not dismiss his character this lightly. There is a hint here that Claudius may owe something of his throne to

Polonius

the support of Polonius in the past, and in Act 2, scene 2 ('Hath there been such a time – I would fain know that –/That I have positively said ''Tis so',/ When it prov'd otherwise?') we see that he has in the past proved useful and reliable. Because Shakespeare is exploring human character as well as the role of destiny in the lives of humankind, Polonius – like other characters in the play – is depicted as both an idiosyncratic individual and as a character type.

The character of Polonius is also important as an indicator of the politics of the age in which the play is set. The superficial tone of the Danish court appears orderly, civilised and polite with recognition given to the importance of decorative, gracious speech (parodied in Polonius and Osric), the relevance of education (suggested by the references to the scholarly pursuits of Hamlet, Rosencrantz and Guildenstern), and an appreciation of the traditional courtly pleasures provided by travelling players and pastimes such as wagering and

Order and Disorder

fencing. But in fact the court of Claudius is full of the treachery and political intrigue which were considered in Shakespeare's time to be a common feature of the fifteenth- and sixteenth-century Italian states about which Machiavelli wrote in *The Prince*. In such courts plotting and assassination (especially by poison) were almost routine and rule by a kind of chaotic despotism was common. Machiavelli argued that strong – even repressive – measures by rulers were needed if such states were not to degenerate into a complete breakdown of order and outright anarchy. It is this aspect of the court of Claudius which Marcellus is referring to when

Claudius

he speaks of something being 'rotten' in the state of Denmark, and which would have been instantly recognised by Shakespeare's audience. As head of the state, the king exerts a powerful influence over everything and in the case of Hamlet's father it is abundantly clear that this influence was good, noble, generous and in all respects admirable. In the case of Claudius his evil deeds have corrupted the state and it is therefore justifiable to remove him by force. Shakespeare often considered such issues in his plays and reflections about the abuse of power and whether it was ever legitimate to remove a 'bad' king are common in his work – compare, for example, the character of Claudius to that of Macbeth or Caesar (a more difficult one).

Seems, madam? Nay, it is. I know not 'seems'

Hamlet is distinguished from most of the other characters both by the depth

Appearance and Reality

of his emotional feeling (his father has been dead almost two months and he is still deep in grief) and by his tendency towards dramatic – almost sensational – behaviour. Notice how in his conversation with his mother there is a stark contrast between what he says and his own behaviour. Is Hamlet himself more concerned here with appearance than reality? Is he, as his mother and Claudius believe, wearing his heart upon his sleeve in public? Fifty-three lines later on, in his soliloquy, he reveals the depth of his torment. In the play's first few scenes Hamlet's true feelings are exposed only to the audience and the Ghost. To other characters – Polonius, Rosencrantz and Guildenstern, and even his mother – he delivers his 'antic disposition' and talks in a stream of cryptic riddles. Characteristically, Hamlet's opaque language is filled with many striking and ironic images of arresting clarity which play upon the difference between appearance and reality. This is a feature of the play – nothing is ever completely what it seems.

Although there are many relationships between characters within the play, none is more important than that between Hamlet and Claudius. The struggle between these two is what the play is all about at heart and a good way to follow this is to look at the plotting and counter-plotting which goes on (or which has already gone on) and which leads to the death of nine of the main characters. As the play opens it

Hamlet

is clear that Claudius has successfully schemed to gain the crown and possibly, before that, his brother's wife. In an attempt to trap Claudius, Hamlet plans 'The Mousetrap'. In return, Claudius plots against Hamlet and sends him to England with his own death warrant, but the plan fails. Claudius then plots with Laertes to arrange a supposedly friendly fencing match which uses a poisoned sword and poisoned wine. This

Claudius

second plot does not work properly and although Hamlet is killed, so are Gertrude, Laertes and Claudius. Only Fortinbras is left to carry on the stewardship of the nation. One key to understanding *Hamlet* lies in recognising that it is an intensely political play, which is about the intrigue surrounding the gaining of power, and its use and abuse, as much as it is about anything else.

O that this too too sullied flesh would melt...

Hamlet is depicted as being still in the early stages of grief, when ordinary life seems meaningless and flat in the face of pain and a sense of loss. His father is never talked about except as an ideal king, noble and righteous and even before Hamlet meets the Ghost and is told about his father's murder he is distressed by his mother's hurried marriage to Claudius. The imagery of an unweeded garden appears frequently in the play, symbolising how the ordered, tended state can become overgrown by rank weeds – such as Claudius – if not carefully nurtured. The growth of weeds is therefore linked in the imagery with the way moral and physical disease can corrupt and decay the fabric of the state and the human body. Hamlet feels burdened with disgust by the inheritance of the flesh and by the weaknesses

Order and Disorder

to which it is heir. He feels corrupted and betrayed by the way his mother's affections have been transferred with 'most wicked speed' from his father to his uncle.

My father's spirit – in arms! All is not well

Alone on the stage, Hamlet confides to the audience his misgivings about the Ghost's appearance. Although we do not yet know the content of the Ghost's message, Hamlet 'doubts' (suspects) some foul play. Traditionally, ghosts appeared to reveal some crime or other and so ending the scene in this way builds tension.

Act 1 Scene 3

Laertes is about to leave for France and warns his sister Ophelia about her feelings for Hamlet. He advises her that although Hamlet may declare his love for her, she must be careful because, as heir to the throne, he is not free to marry whomever he wishes. Polonius arrives and says farewell to his son, but lectures him about how he should behave whilst away. Polonius then reinforces his son's advice to Ophelia, that she should be more wary in her relationships with Hamlet. Polonius tells Ophelia to keep more to herself and forbids her to see Hamlet again.

I shall th'effect of this good lesson keep...

Laertes is comically like his father Polonius, in being keen to give moralising

Ophelia

advice to others, even when motivated by the normal love of a brother for his sister. Ironically, it is Ophelia's obedience in this matter which contributes in part to Hamlet's increasing sense of isolation and thereby to the coming tragedy. Here Ophelia gently rebukes Laertes in case he risks not always taking the same advice which he hands out so freely. Later we see how of all people, Laertes is in no position to counsel others about being wary of the real motives of others.

Ay, springes to catch woodcocks

Polonius orders Ophelia not to see Hamlet again. In Shakespeare's day far

Polonius

greater obedience was expected of children than is customary today and so Ophelia's unprotesting compliance with her father's instructions should not surprise us. Polonius' instruction also serves to increase the sense of isolation surrounding Hamlet. Later we see in Ophelia's madness and supposed suicide the effects of the murder of her father by her own lover, and the damage done between her and Hamlet both by her obedience to her father and by the sins of Gertrude. Both here and in the advice given by Laertes, we see emphasised the notion that sexual passion can seduce the will. Although Polonius is tiresome in his manner, his advice is therefore well given, for it hints at a reason for Gertrude's behaviour with Claudius – a hint which the Ghost subsequently substantiates. The Ghost and Polonius are both fathers who give advice to their sons on how to conduct themselves in an imperfect world. The advice of Polonius, that Laertes should 'to thine own self be true', is ironic coming as it does from one who seems to spend almost all his time plotting and spying. But later this advice provides the key motivation for Laertes and encapsulates the injunction which the Ghost gives to Hamlet: to remember him but not to 'let thy soul contrive against thy mother aught.' Polonius also points out another important aspect of the play,

Appearance and Reality

which is the contrast between appearance and reality. This is reflected here, as elsewhere, by the tortuous language which he uses in his attempts to show his wit but which often result in him being over-clever and tiresome. Conversely, compare the sentiments Polonius expresses here ('Beware of entrance to a quarrel...') with similar ones in Hamlet's speeches, especially that at the end of Act 4, scene 4.

Act 1 Scene 4

Hamlet, Horatio and Marcellus are on the castle walls at midnight when the Ghost again appears. It beckons for Hamlet to follow it, as though it wishes to speak to him alone. Although his friends try to stop him, Hamlet leaves with the Ghost, followed by his friends.

The King doth wake tonight and takes his rouse

Hamlet comments on the drunkenness for which Denmark is becoming

Order and Disorder

known, noting that as with individual men, 'the stamp of one defect' in their nature undermines all their good qualities. The implication is that something is indeed rotten in the state and it is ironic that Claudius should be celebrating his power and position at the moment when the Ghost appears to begin the process of his destruction. Again we are reminded of the contrast between the regal appearance of the King and the drunkard it conceals. The question suggested here is what we might conclude to be the 'one defect' in the different characters of Hamlet, Gertrude, Claudius, Polonius and so on. Critics have sometimes argued that Hamlet lacks resolve, that Gertrude has been too easily ruled by sexual passion, that Claudius gave in to his ambition and that Polonius cannot desist from meddling inquisitiveness. But the text offers evidence both for and against each of these, and other, conclusions and you must weigh the evidence for yourself. You should take account of the interpretations of others in these matters, but providing the text will support your argument, settle for your own.

Angels and ministers of grace defend us!

With the sound of the present king's ordnance still ringing across the stage, the old king makes his appearance, heralding the fate also awaiting Claudius. The tormented world of the spirit which the Ghost inhabits and describes to Hamlet contrasts with the world of physical pleasure and worldly power revelled in by Claudius. Hamlet calls for holy protection because he is unsure of the Ghost's true nature, which is an ironic twist to the theme of appearance and reality.

Appearance and Reality

My fate cries out

Hamlet's cry here is the key to the action of the play. His progress in understanding that it is his fate which cries out to him is what largely determines the pace of the resulting action. Marcellus notes that 'something is rotten in the state of Denmark' and Horatio emphasises an underlying theme of the play when he observes that 'heaven will direct' the resulting course of action.

Hamlet

Act 1 Scene 5

The Ghost identifies itself to Hamlet as his father, and tells him that he must revenge his murder. The Ghost explains how Claudius seduced the Queen, Gertrude, and then poisoned him whilst he was sleeping in his orchard. The Ghost commands Hamlet to avenge his murder but tells him to leave his mother to heaven. The Ghost departs and Hamlet swears to avenge him. When Horatio and Marcellus return they find Hamlet's behaviour very strange. Hamlet makes them swear to keep the events of the night a secret, however strangely he behaves in future.

Mark me

The Ghost speaks for the first time, in a scene whose stillness contrasts with the wild action at the end of the previous one.

...Doom'd for a certain term to walk the night

The Ghost explains that its fate is sealed in Purgatory, a place to which many Elizabethans believed the souls of the dead were condemned if they died without confessing and repenting their sins. Purgatory was a place of eternal fire and pain where sins were slowly burnt away until the soul was purified.

Ay, that incestuous, that adulterate beast

The Ghost speaks of Gertrude as the 'seeming virtuous' queen and emphasises both the corrosive effect of lust over even a 'radiant angel' and the power of Claudius' 'traitorous gifts'. Gertrude is described in terms which emphasise her part as the victim of her own frailty and Hamlet is told to leave her retribution to heaven. You should be alert to the symbolism

Gertrude

of the play: the description of the king poisoned whilst asleep in the garden echoes the biblical story of the Garden of Eden (Denmark), with the serpent's role as evil spirit given to Claudius, leading to the Fall ('something is rotten…').

O all you host of heaven! O earth! What else?

Revenge

The cosmic scale of Hamlet's torment is emphasised in this speech, as is his sense of losing any reference point from which to understand how he should act. Equally the disjointed short lines – the 'wild and whirling words' – which appear when Hamlet is reunited with his friends emphasise the rapid changes of feeling which characterise his near-hysteria. The revenge demanded by the Ghost forces Hamlet to do evil as part of achieving good. The Ghost may be good, but also may be the Devil, just as a man 'may smile, and smile, and be a villain'.

These are but wild and whirling words, my lord

Hamlet

Horatio here touches upon something we see several times in the play from Hamlet – outbursts of behaviour and speech which seem deranged and unreasoned. Hamlet's humorous exchanges with the Ghost might be an expression of his horror and astonishment, or of his confusion about how much to reveal of what he has been told.

Ah ha, boy say'st thou so? Art thou there, truepenny?

The Fool

The Elizabethan audience traditionally associated the area under the stage with dramatic representations of hell. The Ghost's repeated orders from 'the cellarage', together with Hamlet's jocular exchanges with him as he moved around under the ground – *hic et ubique*, 'here and everywhere' in Latin – and the repeated 'swearings' of the oath, would all have contributed to the audience's suspicion about whether this was indeed an 'honest ghost'. The scene, which can powerfully suggest the chaos threatening to overwhelm humankind's attempt to order the world, requires careful playing if it is not to descend into farce for modern audiences.

The time is out of joint. O cursed spite,
That ever I was born to set it right.

Hamlet

At the end of Act 1 we find Hamlet cast as tragic hero, not as the traditional revenger, because of his awareness that the Ghost has committed him to evil in the interests of good. Hamlet's sensitivity to the wonder of the world and the god-like faculties of humankind serve as the bed upon which his duty to the Ghost is his torture. In the 'rottenness' of the state in Denmark it is Hamlet's nobility which becomes his tragic flaw.

Self-test (Questions) Act One

Uncover the plot

Delete some of the alternatives given, to find the correct plot. Beware possible misconceptions and muddles.

The castle sentinels Horatio/Barnardo/Marcellus/Francisco/Reynaldo witness the ghost of the dead king, which appears at dawn/cock crow/midnight. The new king Voltemand/Claudius/Fortinbras has recently married Gertrude/Niobe/Ophelia, his brother's cousin/sister/wife. The new king has sent a message to the King of England/France/Norway to ask his help in calming the warlike ambitions of Fortinbras/Cornelius/Francisco. The King and Queen do not want Hamlet to go back to France/Denmark/Wittenberg, where he has been ambassador/learning to fence/studying, although the son of Reynaldo/Polonius/Horatio is given leave to go back to his studies in France. Laertes warns his sister/cousin/mother Gertrude/Ophelia/Niobe about Hamlet. Polonius/Hamlet/Claudius lectures his son about how he should behave whilst away. Gertrude/Laertes/Polonius forbids Ophelia to see Hamlet again. That night in his room/on the castle walls/whilst at prayers the Ghost again appears and beckons for Hamlet to follow it. The Ghost explains how first Voltemand/Fortinbras/Claudius seduced the Queen, and then poisoned/stabbed/strangled him whilst he was sleeping. The Ghost commands Hamlet to avenge his murder but tells him not to harm Ophelia/not to tell anyone/not to harm his mother. The Ghost departs and Hamlet makes the others swear to help him/keep the events of the night a secret/not harm the Ghost.

Who? What? Why? When? Where? How?

1   Who says the defining characteristic of women is frailty?
2   For what indulgence does Hamlet say that Denmark has become notorious?
3   What, after the funeral of King Hamlet, 'did coldly furnish forth the marriage tables'?
4   Why must the Ghost walk at night and spend its days trapped in fire?
5   To whom does Hamlet confide his secret that he will adopt an 'antic disposition'?
6   The Ghost wears armour from head to foot, so how does Horatio know it is Hamlet's father?
7   According to Hamlet, how long was the gap between his father's death and his mother's remarriage?
8   Who says of Hamlet 'with a larger tether may he walk/Than may be given you.', and to whom?
9   At about what hour does the Ghost appear on both occasions in Act 1?
10 In which scene does the Ghost first speak? What is the last thing it says in Act 1?

Who said that?

1   Seems, madam? Nay, it is. I know not 'seems'.
2   O that this too too sullied flesh would melt,…
3   Springes to catch woodcocks.

4   Angels and ministers of grace defend us!

5   Something is rotten in the state of Denmark.

6   Leave her to heaven,…

7   These are but wild and whirling words…

8   …in the morn and liquid dew of youth/Contagious blastments are most imminent.

9   A little more than kin, and less than kind.

10   I'll cross it though it blast me.

Open quotes

Identify the scene; complete the phrase; identify the speaker and the character being spoken to.

1   But look, the morn in russet mantle clad…

2   The head is not more native to the heart,/The hand more instrumental to the mouth,…

3   For they are actions that a man might play;/But…

4   How weary, stale, flat,…

5   This above all: to thine own self be true…

6   I with wings as swift/As meditation or the thoughts of love…

7   So lust, though to a radiant angel link'd,/Will sate itself in…

8   My tables. Meet it is I set it down…

9   The time is out of…

Act 2 Scene 1

Polonius instructs Reynaldo, who is going to visit Laertes, to spy upon him by suggesting to those he meets that Laertes behaves like a wild-spirited young man, hoping that the others he speaks to will agree. By this devious means Polonius hopes to learn the truth about how his son is conducting himself whilst away from home. After Reynaldo leaves, Ophelia enters and Polonius learns that Hamlet has visited her and has behaved very strangely. Polonius is convinced that Hamlet's behaviour is due to his love for Ophelia and the fact that she has refused to see him lately, following his orders. Polonius decides to tell Claudius.

And then, sir, does a this – a does – what was I about to say? By the mass, I was about to say something.

Polonius keeps losing his place in his own thoughts, in a parody of the effect

The Fool

he has on other characters and that which Hamlet has on him on several occasions. Although this underlines the fool-like, bumbling side of his character, it also reveals the calculating side of him which wishes to control every aspect of the behaviour of others, including his son, Laertes, and his daughter, Ophelia. Notice how he is quite happy for Reynaldo to spy and to lie if it achieves what he wishes and in this respect Polonius is shown to be a lesser echo of Claudius. This underlines the way spying and intrigue run through the action of the play.

32

Lord Hamlet, with his doublet all unbrac'd...

Ophelia here describes Hamlet as acting out the melodramatic picture of grief

Appearance and Reality

which he disdained in Act 1 when talking to his mother ('I know not 'seems'.) In his verbal fencing with Polonius in scene 2 Hamlet manipulates their conversation in the same way as he here manipulates the way he appears to Ophelia. Both are designed to draw the audience's attention to the effects of Hamlet's new way of behaving. Hamlet manipulates verbal and physical appearance until the genuine play-actors arrive later in the play and only then becomes himself again. Notice here how the behaviour of Polonius is different to that when he spoke to Reynaldo. Later, in the speech beginning: 'That hath made him mad', Polonius ironically admits that his own jealousy has led him to be over-suspicious and devious. These same characteristics will be the agents of his own undoing.

Act 2 Scene 2

The King and Queen welcome Rosencrantz and Guildenstern, Hamlet's friends from university at Wittenberg. They agree to help the King and Queen in their attempts to discover the cause of Hamlet's recent behaviour. Voltemand and Cornelius return from Norway with news that Fortinbras has been made to promise to behave peaceably towards Denmark. Fortinbras has been instructed to go with his army and fight the Poles and the Norwegian King seeks permission for safe passage for them through Denmark. Polonius explains to the King and Queen that he believes Hamlet's madness to be due to Ophelia rejecting his love. He produces letters to Ophelia from Hamlet and gets the King and Queen to agree to setting a trap to test his conclusions. Left alone, Polonius talks to Hamlet who has appeared reading a book, but he receives only insults and puzzling replies to his questions. As Polonius also leaves, Rosencrantz and Guildenstern arrive and Hamlet makes it clear that he knows they have been sent to observe him. A travelling group of players arrive and Hamlet welcomes them, asking one of them to recite a favourite speech he remembers hearing before. As the players go into the castle, Hamlet agrees with one of them the play he wishes to see performed for the court and arranges for some lines of his own to be specially inserted. When alone on stage, Hamlet criticises himself for his delay in avenging the Ghost and plans to use the players to expose the King's guilt, thereby satisfying himself that the Ghost spoke the truth.

Madam, I swear I use no art at all

The Fool

Polonius keeps overcomplicating what he is trying to say and thus obscures his message and makes his audience impatient. He is pompous and vain, as well as long-winded, and his impressive-sounding speeches actually consist of very little. Although Polonius clearly thinks of himself as clever and intellectual he is in fact superficial, clumsy and often in error in his judgement. He is here being used as a parody of a stock comic figure in Elizabethan drama who uses complicated flowery expressions, but the effect is to make the audience more affectionate towards him and thus more shocked by his eventual killing. Notwithstanding his protestations to the contrary, Polonius actually uses considerable 'art' in his attempts to control others.

Hath there been such a time...
That I have positively said "Tis so',
When it prov'd otherwise?

Polonius

Polonius counts himself a master at observing others but his overconfidence in his own abilities is his undoing. In spite of all his well-meaning advice to others, it is clear that Polonius consistently gets it wrong in seeing Hamlet's madness as lovesickness. There is unconscious irony in his conceited bragging about taking his head from his shoulders if he is in error. Gertrude has been nearer the truth in saying to Claudius that Hamlet's behaviour is more to do with 'his father's death and our o'er-hasty marriage'.

At such a time I'll loose my daughter to him

Polonius uses 'loose' in the mating or farmyard sense, and thereby does his own character little good in the eyes of the audience. His tendency to abuse others – even those he loves – for his own scheming purposes identifies him with the rottenness which Hamlet sees in Denmark.

Pol. Do you know me, my Lord?
Ham. Excellent well. You are a fishmonger

Hamlet mercilessly exploits the intellectual failings of Polonius by pretending to be mad. The imagery of a fishmonger is, on the surface, completely inappropriate and therefore comic. Hamlet turns it into a reference to the

Sex, Love and Marriage

alleged tendency for the daughters of fishmongers to breed rapidly and links it to images of the sun (a reference to the King or Prince) breeding maggots in dead meat – a common Elizabethan superstition. Beneath the surface it also echoes the desire of Polonius to 'loose' his daughter, as in Elizabethan times a 'fishwife' was often a bawdy reference to a prostitute, and the 'fishmonger' therefore was supported by her earnings. References to his mother's incest with Claudius are also just beneath the surface of Hamlet's language here, although displaced onto Ophelia.

Appearance and Reality

Hamlet's display of his 'antic disposition' and the arrival of the players are examples of the contrast between appearance and reality which appears often in the action. Claudius and

Polonius have both pretended to be something which they are not and now Hamlet begins to turn their own weapon against them.

My excellent good friends

Hamlet greets his old childhood and school friends warmly and is clearly pleased to see them. By the time we reach Act 3, scene 2 his feelings have turned to ones of distrust as he accuses them of wanting to 'play upon' him like a musical instrument. Eventually he sends them to their death with no feelings of remorse.

I have of late, but wherefore I know not, lost all my mirth...

Hamlet

For Hamlet the world has become a 'sterile promontory', the air a 'foul and pestilent congregation of vapours' and the noble majesty of mankind a 'quintessence of dust'. The overgrown garden, filled with weeds, dominated by 'things rank and gross in nature', and the poisoned and lifeless world, are reflections of Hamlet's feelings about his mother and Claudius. They are also part of the play's philosophical concern with relationships between heaven and earth, the right qualities for a king and the disordered state into which the world is thrown when God's will is not executed. The disorder which has overtaken Hamlet's life is an echo of the larger disorder

Order and
Disorder

which is afflicting the entire universe, to which reference is made in many parts of the play. The importance of maintaining the correct balance between different elements in the body is a central part of Elizabethan views about human well-being, where the 'humours' needed to exist in the correct proportions, otherwise melancholy or other illness resulted. In the same way the Elizabethan view of the world-order hinged upon humankind maintaining the correct relationship with God in the stewardship of His creation. The dual nature of humankind is part beast/part spiritual creature, part devil/part angel. Hamlet, as an agent of revenge, therefore has as his purpose the releasing of his father's spirit from purgatory and also the restoring of order in the world.

Yet Hamlet is also playing with his two school-friends. Just as he pretended to Polonius that he was lovesick for Ophelia, so here he adopts the pose of the melancholy man. Evidence that his friends may be aware of some lightness in his tone can be seen in their laughter.

He that plays the king shall be welcome...

Appearance
and Reality

The introduction of the professional players again emphasises the importance of the theme of appearance and reality and prepares us for the key role which the players will have in developing the plot. We already know of the 'welcome' which Hamlet wishes to give to 'he that plays the king' and this phrase also underlines the importance of Hamlet's false behaviour, his 'disposition', as a means to discover the truth. It is against this complex backdrop that Hamlet later falls to a discussion with the players of the falseness of ham-acting. The discussion about the 'little eyases' (young hawks) is a topical reference to the furore being caused at the time by the use of child actors on the Elizabethan stage, but at a subtler level this discussion also hints at the shifting allegiances which we have seen at work in Denmark.

O Jephthah, judge of Israel, what a treasure hadst thou!

Hamlet has confessed to his school-friends that he feigns madness when it

Ophelia

suits him – when the wind is 'north-north west' – and when Polonius arrives with his tiresome and long-winded introduction of the players he resumes his pretence. But Hamlet's words are again laced with dramatic irony, for the biblical Jephthah sacrificed his virgin daughter in the same way that Polonius unthinkingly sacrifices Ophelia, although Jephthah's daughter bemoaned her virginity in a way which is paralleled by Hamlet's mocking in the present play.

I heard thee speak me a speech once...

In asking the player to recite a speech Hamlet introduces the first of the 'plays

Revenge

within the play'. Hamlet plays the classical revenger, Pyrrhus, as an amateur actor, though Polonius notes that he takes the part 'with good accent and good discretion'. This marks his growth into the role in reality but also separates him from the traditional revenger role adopted later by Laertes. By such devices Shakespeare continuously invites the audience to consider the differing types of revenge and to question their moral validity. Hamlet's request for a particular play to be performed, with additional lines penned by him, again reminds us of the use of deception to discover truth and Polonius' instructions to Reynaldo: 'by indirections find directions out'.

O what a rogue and peasant slave am I!

The actor in the play has summoned up what seem to be real feelings of grief

Hamlet

and agony, and 'all for nothing', whilst Hamlet seems unable to act even in the face of real evil. Hamlet knows he must put aside his 'antic disposition' and bend himself to real action, and in this soliloquy he spurs himself on. Hamlet admits he has a theatrical side to his character and, interestingly, he decides to use the appearance of reality – the play – as a catalyst for real action. He also intends to use the play to test whether the spirit he has seen is but the Devil in a 'pleasing shape', again reminding us of the theme of appearance and reality in the play and echoing his earlier comment that 'one may smile, and smile, and be a villain'.

Self-test (Questions) Act Two

Uncover the plot
Delete some of the alternatives given, to find the correct plot. Beware possible misconceptions and muddles.

Claudius/Hamlet/Polonius instructs Reynaldo, who is going to visit Laertes/ Horatio/Voltemand, to spy upon him. Gertrude/Ophelia/The Ghost says that Hamlet has been behaving very strangely. Polonius is convinced that this is because of the Ghost/his love for Ophelia/his mother's marriage. The King and Queen welcome Hamlet's friends from Wittenberg/England/Elsinore. Messengers return with news that the Norwegian/Danish/English King now seeks permission for safe passage for his army through Denmark. Claudius/Horatio/Polonius produces letters to Gertrude/Ophelia from Laertes/Hamlet and gets the King and Queen to agree to setting a trap for him. Hamlet says he knows that his friends have been sent to observe him/cheer him up/go to England with him. A travelling group of players arrive and Claudius/Hamlet/Horatio welcomes them. The players agree to include some lines by Hamlet/Horatio/Polonius to be added into their play for the court. When alone on stage, Claudius/Polonius/Hamlet criticises himself for his delay/his sins/his suspicions.

Who? What? Why? When? Where? How?
1 Who 'was about to say something'?
2 Name Hamlet's two school friends.
3 What convinces Polonius that Hamlet's madness is due to love-sickness?
4 Why does Ophelia give Polonius Hamlet's love letters to her?
5 What task is Reynaldo given?
6 To what two things does the Queen attribute Hamlet's apparent madness?
7 What, to Hamlet, is 'this quintessence of dust'?
8 Who gives whom three thousand crowns annually and for what?
9 Hamlet says he could be 'bounded in a nutshell and count myself a king of infinite space', were it not for what thing?
10 Who thinks of whom as 'faithful and honourable'?

Who said that?
1 ...brevity is the soul of wit
2 You are a fishmonger.
3 As 'twere a thing a little soil'd i'th' working
4 Happy in that we are not over-happy...
5 but there is, sir, an eyrie of children, little eyases,...
6 What's Hecuba to him, or he to her...
7 Denmark's a prison.
8 At such a time I'll loose my daughter to him.
9 and the devil hath power/T'assume a pleasing shape...
10 As if he had been loosed out of hell/To speak of horrors, he comes before me.

Open quotes
Identify the scene; complete the phrase; identify the speaker and the character being spoken to.
1 With windlasses and with assays of bias,
2 ...for there is nothing either good or bad...
3 I have of late, but wherefore I know not,...
4 Though this be madness,...

Act 3 Scene 1

The King and Polonius hide to watch the meeting of Hamlet and Ophelia which they have arranged. When Hamlet appears he reflects upon the purpose of life and, seeing Ophelia, criticises her and all women for their falseness. Ophelia is convinced that Hamlet has gone mad. After Hamlet leaves, the King says he will send him to England for his own good, as he believes there is more to Hamlet's behaviour than Polonius supposes. The King agrees to a suggestion by Polonius that he should spy on another meeting, this time between Hamlet and the Queen, to make sure that Hamlet's madness is not caused by lovesickness.

Ophelia, walk you here

Claudius

As Polonius instructs his obedient daughter his comment that 'pious action' and appearance may 'sugar o'er the devil himself' stings Claudius, whose comment in an aside is the first evidence we have, apart from that supplied by the Ghost, of his guilt.

To be, or not to be, that is the question…

Order and Disorder

Some critics have seen this soliloquy as an echo of that in Act 1, scene 2 ('O that this too too sullied flesh would melt') and therefore as a consideration by Hamlet of suicide. Others have argued that such a conclusion makes little dramatic sense, for Hamlet now has every reason to want to live, because he has a device by which he feels he can catch the King. This soliloquy therefore may be seen as an extension of his last one and a further stiffening of his resolve to avenge his father's murder. Notice Hamlet's interesting comment about no 'traveller' ever returning from 'the undiscover'd country' (the land of the dead) and consider what light you think this sheds on the way he feels about the Ghost.

Get thee to a nunnery

Hamlet

Is it possible to explain Hamlet's attitude to Ophelia here as a result only of his loss of faith in people? Is Hamlet displacing onto Ophelia the guilt he sees in his mother and his rejection of her? It is difficult otherwise to explain Hamlet's behaviour here, unless we agree with Ophelia's 'O, what a noble mind is here o'erthrown!' Or is Hamlet's gross rudeness deliberate because he suspects that they are being watched?

Ophelia describes all the noble characteristics which Hamlet possesses and which combined to make him an ideal man, but which have now been spoiled by the madness she sees in him. Hamlet seems repelled by sex because it produces more life, which brings more evil into the world as an inextricable part of human character. Hamlet's revulsion is heightened by the way his mother has entered into an incestuous and adulterous relationship, where the attractions of the flesh have led her into betraying his father's memory. This explains Hamlet's obsession with his mother's 'incestuous sheets' not, as some critics have imagined, as some kind of obsession with his own mother as an object of sexual desire. It is unnecessary to invent an Oedipus complex for Hamlet in order to understand the way he treats the women in the play.

Sex, Love and Marriage

Polonius has abused his daughter to gain favour with Claudius, causing the audience to question his worth as a caring parent. This marks the turning point in the fortunes of Polonius' family as they are in turn sacrificed to the will of Claudius. According to the Ghost, the corrupting guile of Claudius has turned the head of the Queen; on several occasions we see it poured into receptive ears just as poisonously as the 'leperous distilment' which he used upon King Hamlet, sleeping in the orchard.

Claudius

O, what a noble mind is here o'erthrown!

Ophelia emphasises Hamlet's princely qualities by speaking what is almost an epitaph for them, now that his behaviour towards her suggests that he has become mad. Compare this scene with Act 4, scene 5, where Ophelia sings scraps of folk songs about the loss of a loved one through death or desertion. Whilst she is aware here of what she has lost in Hamlet, we never hear described an equal recognition from him of everything in her which he loved before the action of the play opened.

Hamlet

Act 3 Scene 2

Hamlet instructs the players in the art of acting, warning them of the dangers of overacting their parts and thereby ruining the effect. As the players leave, Horatio comes in and Hamlet asks him to watch the King's reactions during the play that evening. The court arrives to see the play 'The Mousetrap', during which the Player-Queen vows never to marry again if the Player-King dies. Following this the Player-King sleeps and another actor, playing the nephew, pours poison in the Player-King's ear. Hamlet announces that in the next part of the play the nephew gets the love of the Player-King's wife. Claudius leaves the play abruptly and Hamlet is convinced this is evidence of his guilt. Rosencrantz and Guildenstern bring a message to Hamlet that the King is distressed and the Queen wishes to see him. Hamlet rounds on them in anger, mocks them and accuses them of trying to manipulate him. When Polonius arrives with the same request from the Queen, Hamlet is equally scornful of him, mocking his obsequious manner. They leave Hamlet alone and although he feels his anger and passion to be at their height, he vows not to use physical violence towards his mother as he goes off to see her.

Full thirty times hath Phoebus' cart gone round
Neptune's salt wash and Tellus' orbed ground

When the players are performing they speak in rhyming couplets, but otherwise they speak, as do others of their social status, in prose. Shakespeare uses prose as an indicator of the lower status of a speaker or event, such as a letter, or a servant or messenger. Otherwise blank verse is used extensively in the play. This unrhymed but rhythmically regular language is used to reflect a speaker of superior social status, so that, for example, whilst the grave-digger can say: 'Give me leave. Here lies the water – good. Here stands the man – good.', we find Hamlet expressing himself in more measured language: ' 'Tis now the very witching time of night,/When churchyards yawn and hell itself breathes out/Contagion to this world.'

No, no, they do but jest – poison in jest

Hamlet's pointed remark reveals to the audience that Claudius begins to suspect that he is the target, and that Hamlet has indeed arranged for there to be poison in his jesting.

You are as good as a chorus, my lord

Ophelia's comment alerts us to the way in which Hamlet's 'Mousetrap' is

Sex, Love and Marriage

indeed a kind of chorus upon the events which have preceded the action of the play, but from which its development arises. Similarly Hamlet's coarse banter with Ophelia, especially as it pointedly follows his earlier rejection of her, acts as a commentary upon the players' presentation of his mother's sexual betrayal. Hamlet shows himself acutely aware of other betrayals later, when he accuses Rosencrantz and Guildenstern of trying to play him like an instrument and then, in his tormenting of Polonius, proceeds to call the tune to which the sycophantic courtier dances.

'Tis now the very witching time of night...

Hamlet

Hamlet says his resolution is now firm and his purpose clear. He could 'drink hot blood' but will confine his violence towards his mother to speaking in daggers. He will be cruel towards her, but not 'unnatural' in his deeds unlike those committed by Claudius, who seduced Hamlet's mother and murdered his father.

Act 3 Scene 3

Claudius tells Rosencrantz and Guildenstern that Hamlet must go immediately with them to England. Polonius says Hamlet is going to meet Gertrude and so he will hide behind the arras to overhear what is said. After the King is left alone, he confesses his murder but says he cannot see how forgiveness can be his, for he still possesses all the things which he gained: the crown, the Queen and his ambition. As the King kneels to pray Hamlet appears and, unseen, draws his sword and considers killing him but decides against it. Hamlet thinks that the King might go to heaven, unlike his own father who is condemned to purgatory, and so decides instead to kill Claudius when he is full of sin so that his soul would go to hell. Hamlet thinks this would then complete the revenge.

O, my offence is rank, it smells to heaven...

Claudius

Claudius here admits that his crime 'hath the primal eldest curse upon't' – in that he has imitated Cain, who the Bible depicts as the first criminal, in murdering his own brother. References to Cain also appear in Act 1, scene 2 and Act 5, scene 1, as reminders of this connection. Notice the contrast between the confident monarch we see elsewhere in the play and the character who is here ridden with guilt and uncertain of himself. This is a complex example of the juxtaposition of reality and appearance which runs through the play, because after Hamlet has decided to spare him we discover that the 'words' of Claudius may well 'fly up' but will not go to heaven as real prayers because they are not supported by his thoughts and real intentions. Subsequently he shows no signs at all of being prepared to forsake any of the gains he has made through his sinful actions.

Appearance
and Reality

Notice how often the play makes use of 'watching' as a dramatic device; we are shown different characters secretly observing each other as a way for us (and them) to divine the truth. Here Hamlet watches Claudius, who seems to be praying. Polonius spies on Hamlet and Ophelia, later he spies on Hamlet and Gertrude. Rosencrantz and Guildenstern are sent to spy on Hamlet, but he reverses the subterfuge by opening the secret letter they carry to England. The Ghost watches over the castle at the start of the play and later on monitors the behaviour of Gertrude and of Hamlet and comments upon it. Hamlet watches the King during the players' performance, in order to trap him. This use of 'watching' within the play dramatises the contrast between appearance and reality and the way many characters are deceiving themselves, or trying to deceive others, in different ways. All of the major characters are shown at various times as either deceiving themselves about their own situation, or are shown as deliberately attempting to deceive others.

Now might I do it pat, now a is a-praying

Hamlet decides not to kill Claudius here because he is in prayer and to do so

Revenge

would send him to heaven, when Hamlet wishes him to spend an eternity suffering in purgatory. Hamlet's calculated cruelty here is echoed later on in the way he deals with Rosencrantz and Guildenstern and has been interpreted as the justice of 'an eye for an eye', given what the Ghost has told him. But notice the dramatic irony in Claudius being unable to pray whilst Hamlet is unwilling to kill him because he thinks Claudius is praying. The audience are also deceived by the action, until Hamlet has gone and it is too late for him to overhear Claudius' revelation that he could not pray. Some critics interpret this scene as an example of Hamlet's unnecessary delay in fulfilling the Ghost's instructions, but the text here does not support such a conclusion. Note that Hamlet has the traditional revenger's problem to contend with; he can only punish the offence of murder by committing the same crime himself and, as we see later in the play, must therefore accept the fate which awaits those who commit evil deeds.

Act 3 Scene 4

Polonius tells Gertrude that he will hide behind a curtain to overhear her conversation with Hamlet, but he cries out as the Queen becomes frightened at Hamlet's anger, and Hamlet thrusts his rapier through the curtain and kills him. Hamlet then criticises his mother for being involved in killing his father and for marrying Claudius. As Gertrude becomes more upset, the Ghost enters and when Hamlet falls to talking to it she is convinced he is mad. But he tells her he only feigns madness and makes her promise to keep his secret. He also tries to persuade his mother not to have sex with Claudius in future. Hamlet also tells her that his two untrustworthy school fellows are to accompany him to England and then drags away the body of Polonius.

How now? A rat! Dead for a ducat, dead

Polonius

With these words, Hamlet stabs Polonius through the arras and fatally wounds him. Ironically, Polonius has discovered nothing by his spying but has died for his pains anyway. It is the killing of Polonius which propels the action towards its tragic climax and begins the second revenge plot in the play.

Hamlet

Hamlet manages to frighten his mother so much that she calls for help and his behaviour later causes the Ghost to rebuke him for the way he has treated his mother. Hamlet is concerned with persuading his mother to abandon her ties to Claudius and help him with his plans to trick the King into believing that he is mad—so much so that he seems unconcerned with his murder of Polonius. Why is Hamlet so cool about the murder? There seems no way he could have known who was behind the arras, but clearly he mistook Polonius for the King: 'I took thee for thy better'. But why, if he thought it was Claudius, would he kill him now – when he is not involved in any evil act – in the light of his decision at the end of the last scene when Claudius was at prayer? Or is this a dramatic marking of a change in Hamlet's ability to take swift action? Hamlet's motives are often perplexing and although he is a fascinating and puzzling character he is not

Sex, Love and Marriage

presented as especially likeable. He seems cruel, vindictive and cold towards others on many occasions but can be gentle and loving. Equally, he can be very impulsive but also has a very calculating, introverted side to him. His mother, talking to Claudius later, says that he is 'mad as the sea and wind, when both contend which is the mightier.' Reaching conclusions about Hamlet's state of mind at any point is difficult, not just because he develops emotionally throughout the play, but also because the many sides of his complex character are only partially revealed at different times. Here we have Hamlet engaged in what is clearly an evil act – as the

Revenge

revenger of his father he kills another man's father. Yet the language used distinguishes clearly between Hamlet's impulsive killing of this 'wretched, rash, intruding fool' and the deliberate act of Claudius killing his brother with what the Ghost calls a 'leprous distilment' of 'cursed hebenon' (Act 1, scene 5). However, the complexity of Hamlet's situation is unlike that of the traditional revenger, sweeping heroically and single-mindedly to seek vengeance for an evil murder; instead, he is a character torn by his own feelings who recognises the potential for good and evil in himself and who, in trying to right an existing wrong, commits another himself.

Thou turn'st my eyes into my very soul...

Unlike Claudius, Gertrude shows evidence of real repentance for what she

Gertrude

has done. Here she seems also to agree to support her son in his action against Claudius, which would appear to leave all the major characters deceiving someone. This discussion between mother and son – the only extended one in the play – concentrates upon how her sexual lust has led her to leave a 'wholesome brother' for a 'mildew'd ear'. Note that the murder of old Hamlet is never explicitly mentioned, the implication being that Gertrude was not involved in this act.

A king of shreds and patches...

At these unintentionally ironic words from Hamlet, the Ghost of the old king reappears, not to criticise Hamlet for being too harsh with his mother – the text does not support this interpretation – but to remind him of his true purpose, which it fears is now 'almost blunted'. The Ghost seems to be pointing out that Hamlet is letting time slip by and is allowing his repugnance with his mother's sexual betrayal to deflect him from the true course of revenge.

Following the Ghost's reminder, we see in the rest of this scene increasing hints that Hamlet recognises and accepts the fate which is in store for him, and is now reconciled with his mother and trusts her with his knowledge of how Claudius is attempting to shape events through others.

Hamlet

Self-test (Questions) Act Three

Uncover the plot
Delete some of the alternatives given, to find the correct plot. Beware possible misconceptions and muddles.

The King and Gertrude/Laertes/Polonius hide to watch a meeting of Hamlet and Ophelia. Hamlet criticises all women for their falseness/sexuality/vanity. Ophelia is convinced that Hamlet has gone mad. The King says he will send Laertes/Hamlet to Paris/Wittenberg/England and agrees to let Polonius spy on a meeting between Hamlet and the Queen. Hamlet/Polonius/Horatio instructs the players in the art of acting. Hamlet asks Ophelia/Horatio/Gertrude to watch the King's reactions during the play that evening. Polonius/Claudius/Fortinbras leaves the play abruptly and Hamlet is convinced this is evidence of his guilt. Polonius/Osric/Rosencrantz says the Queen wants to see Hamlet but is mocked for his obsequious manner. Hamlet vows not to use threats/mental torture/physical violence towards his mother as he goes off to see her. Rosencrantz and Guildenstern are told they must go immediately to Denmark/England/Wittenberg. Polonius/Claudius says he will hide behind the arras to spy on Hamlet's meeting with Ophelia/Gertrude. When the King is alone, he confesses he murdered his brother/seduced Gertrude but says he cannot see how forgiveness can be his. As the King tries to sleep/concentrate/pray Hamlet appears and considers killing him but decides against it because he does not trust the Ghost/the King might go to heaven/he cannot bring himself to do it. When Hamlet meets his mother she becomes frightened and Claudius/Polonius cries out; Hamlet kills/wounds him by thrusting his dagger/rapier through the curtain. Hamlet then beats/criticises/threatens his mother for being involved in killing his father and for marrying Polonius/Fortinbras/Claudius. The Ghost appears and Claudius/Hamlet/Polonius talks to it. Gertrude is now convinced Hamlet is mad. Hamlet says he fears he is mad/is only pretending is better now and makes her promise not to sleep with the King again/to obey the Ghost/to keep his secret. Hamlet says he does not trust Polonius/his school fellows/the Ghost and that he is going away to England/Poland/Norway.

Who? What? Why? When? Where? How?
1   To whom does Hamlet confide that he is 'not in madness,/But mad in craft' in what scene and why?
2   The comment from Polonius that 'with devotion's visage/And pious action we do sugar o'er/The devil himself' has what unintended effect?
3   From which country does no traveller ever return?

4   Who says of whom that God has given them one face but they make themselves another?

5   What evidence is there that Hamlet thought the person behind the arras was someone else?

6   Who is described as a 'wretched, rash, intruding fool' and by whom, to whom and on what occasion?

7   Who should not 'saw the air too much' and why?

8   For what reason at first does Hamlet think that the Ghost has returned?

9   Why does Hamlet tell Ophelia to go to a nunnery?

10 What disadvantage does Hamlet see in the otherwise attractive prospect of 'that sleep of death'?

Who said that?

1   I am myself indifferent honest...

2   Words without thoughts never to heaven go.

3   A king of shreds and patches –

4   O, it offends me to the soul to hear a robustious periwig-pated fellow tear a passion to tatters, to very rags...

5   O wretched state! O bosom black as death!/O limed soul, that struggling to be free/Art more engag'd!

6   Give me that man/That is not passion's slave, and I will wear him/In my heart's core...

7   There's something in his soul/O'er which his melancholy sits on brood ...

8   The lady doth protest too much, methinks.

9   A rat! Dead for a ducat, dead.

10 Now could I drink hot blood...

Open quotes

Identify the scene; complete the phrase; identify the speaker and the character being spoken to.

1   I'll take the Ghost's word ...

2   Look here upon this picture, and on this, ...

3   There's letters seal'd, and my two schoolfellows,/Whom I will trust ...

4   To be or not to be, that is the question: ...(complete next four lines)

5   And do not spread the compost on the weeds ...

6   But look, amazement on thy mother sits. (complete next three lines)

7   For 'tis the sport to have the enginer ...

8   Thou turn'st my eyes into my very soul, ...(complete next two lines)

9   O, my offence is rank, ...(complete this and the next two lines)

Act 4 Scene 1

The Queen tells Claudius about Hamlet's killing of Polonius and he notes that it might easily have been him who died had he been there. Claudius tells Rosencrantz and Guildenstern to go and find the body of Polonius.

Mad as the sea and wind when both contend...

Gertrude

Some critics see this scene as evidence that Hamlet's mother is aiding him in his feigned madness, because she keeps her son's secret and seems a little distant from Claudius, others that she is now convinced that he really is mad. You must decide on the balance of probabilities for yourself. Notice how

Claudius seems increasingly concerned for himself and his own safety, again marking him off a little more from Gertrude. This scene and the next three – all short – are used to accelerate the action by the rapid changes of setting and character.

Act 4 Scene 2

Rosencrantz and Guildenstern find Hamlet but he mocks them and will not tell them where he has put the body of Polonius, although he agrees to go with them to see the King.

I understand you not, my lord

Hamlet's antic disposition reappears to both confuse and alienate his former school friends.

Act 4 Scene 3

Claudius discusses with some Lords the fact that although Hamlet is dangerous, he is well liked by the people, and therefore must be treated carefully. Sending Hamlet to England must not appear to be threatening towards him. Hamlet is brought to the court and mocks Claudius. He tells him where he has hidden the body of Polonius and Claudius says he is sending Hamlet to England immediately for his own safety. When everyone else has left, the King reveals that he is also sending a letter with Hamlet in which he threatens to make war on England unless they kill Hamlet for him.

Now, Hamlet, where's Polonius?

The Fool

Hamlet answers the King's questions with derision, hinting menacingly that the King may soon be consumed through the guts of a beggar – that all men share the same fate as his father. Equally he invites Claudius himself to look for Polonius in hell, suggesting that this is where he both belongs and is soon going. Throughout all this, notice Hamlet's increasing concentration on the physical corruption which death leads to, echoing the moral corruption he sees in the court and in Claudius especially. Claudius is clearly desperate to be rid of Hamlet and tells him that, for his own safety, he must depart for England.

So it is, if thou knews't our purposes

Appearance and Reality

Hamlet and Claudius seem here to be fully aware of each other's unspoken ironies – that Claudius' 'purposes' are to kill Hamlet, and that the 'cherub' which sees these purposes may be the Ghost. When left alone, Claudius reveals that his true intentions are indeed to arrange for Hamlet's death.

Act 4 Scene 4

The army of Fortinbras marches across the stage and Hamlet, accompanied by Rosencrantz and Guildenstern, meets one of its captains. The captain reveals that they go to fight over a tiny insignificant piece of land. Left alone, Hamlet wonders that he is so slow to avenge such a great crime as the murder of his father when this army of twenty thousand men is prepared to fight and die for nothing more than honour. He vows that from now on he will have only bloody thoughts.

How all occasions do inform against me...

This soliloquy often presents modern students with a puzzle which goes to the heart of what the play is all about. Hamlet laments his inaction by comparing his situation with that of Fortinbras and his army. For Hamlet has every reason to act, just as the great army before him acts – not just when their survival is threatened (even an animal would act under such circumstances) but for the importance of an idea: 'Rightly to be great is not to stir without great argument, but greatly to find quarrel in a straw when honour's at the stake.' But Hamlet's motive for acting is revenge, so to modern students he seems able to obtain justice for his father only by avenging him in the murder

Revenge

of Claudius. Revenge belongs to an ancient un-Christian moral code which was honoured by many in Shakespeare's time. Hamlet's admiration for the army of Fortinbras is founded upon their willingness to die for mere honour, which is 'a fantasy and trick of fame'. Although Hamlet raises questions about the simple code of honour of Fortinbras and his army, it is clear that what he questions, he also admires.

Hamlet

Hamlet is a noble and rounded character, however, and is more of a Renaissance prince than the stock revenger of Elizabethan melodrama. We see him as a gifted soldier and scholar; an educated courtier with taste who is an informed and critical judge of drama and acting; and a patriot who has a concern for both his own honour and that of his country. He displays courage in facing the Ghost and defeating the pirates, and his torment is not a product of cowardice or inexcusable delay in avenging his father but of his desperate wish to do the right thing. We are prevented from a simplistic and flat conception of his character by these qualities and by the suffering which he endures as a result of the rejection of his own love for his mother and Ophelia and theirs for him.

Act 4 Scene 5

A messenger tells Gertrude that Ophelia is behaving madly, rambling wildly and unhappily in her speech in a way that makes strange sense. Ophelia enters and sings songs about a dead lover. When Claudius appears she sings about a seducer who betrays his lover. As Ophelia leaves she talks strangely about a burial — presumably that of Polonius — and her brother learning about it. A messenger arrives to say that Laertes has arrived with a mob. Laertes bursts in with some followers and demands vengeance for his murdered father. Claudius promises him this, declaring his own innocence. Ophelia enters and sings about a funeral. She gives out flowers and sings about the death of an old man. As she leaves, Claudius tells Laertes that he will help him seek revenge, promising his own life and throne if he is found to be implicated in the death of Polonius.

A document in madness: thoughts and remembrance fitted

Although the 'mad scene' was a stock piece of the theatre of Shakespeare's time (often featuring a woman) it is here used to develop contrasts and emphasise parallels: Ophelia's real madness compared to Hamlet's feigned; and the murder of the fathers of Hamlet and Laertes and the revenging of both.

They bore him bare-fac'd on the bier,
And in his grave rain'd many a tear

Ophelia's grief for her father's death and for the part played in it by her lover

Ophelia

are inextricably linked in her mind. She loved both her father and his murderer and her inability to reconcile the conflict this produces within her, together with Hamlet's rejection of her, is what has driven her mad. Hamlet's wild behaviour is similarly driven by Gertrude loving both his father and his father's murderer. However, Gertrude has succumbed to the bawdy lusts of the outside world, to which Ophelia here refers, but of which she herself has no experience. The flowers she mentions are symbols of important themes within the play and act as commentary upon the behaviour of the main characters: rosemary for remembrance; pansies for sad thoughts; fennel for flattery; and columbine for marital unfaithfulness; rue (the 'herb of grace') for repentance; daisies for unhappy love; and violets for faithfulness – which 'withered all when my father died'. Like her lover Hamlet, Ophelia is a victim of the tragedy that has befallen Denmark. Her madness is timed dramatically to coincide with the return of Laertes, so that the second revenge plot can move forward forcefully.

Act 4 Scene 6

Horatio is brought a letter from Hamlet by some sailors, in which he learns that on his way to England Hamlet was captured by pirates. Rosencrantz and Guildenstern have continued on to England. Hamlet asks Horatio to give to the King the letters which the sailors carry and then hurry to meet him.

Horatio, when thou shalt have overlooked this...

The device of a letter provides a dramatic pause in the action between the 'mad scene' and the following scene of the plotting between Claudius and Laertes. It also emphasises the skill of Hamlet in winning round the pirates and whets the audience's appetite to know what has happened to Rosencrantz and Guildenstern. Notice also the enigmatic echo of the Ghost's words in Hamlet's 'words to speak in thine ear' which will make Horatio 'dumb' with astonishment.

Act 4 Scene 7

Claudius explains to Laertes that he cannot act directly against Hamlet because of how he feels towards Gertrude and because Hamlet is well-liked by the common people. A messenger arrives with a letter from Hamlet, saying that he will come to the King tomorrow and explain his return to Denmark. Claudius and Laertes plot a fencing match between Hamlet and Laertes in which the point of Laertes' sword will be unblunted. Laertes says he will poison the tip of the sword and Claudius says he will poison the wine that Hamlet will be given to quench his thirst during the match. The Queen enters to announce that Ophelia has drowned and Laertes leaves in tears.

The Queen his mother/Lives almost by his looks

Claudius

Claudius here explains to Laertes that he cannot harm Hamlet without hurting Gertrude, for whom he seems to have genuine feelings of love. But this may be only an excuse which Claudius is using as part of a ploy to use Laertes for his own ends. Claudius' conscience is blunted sufficiently for him to have been able to murder his brother and to attempt to have his brother's son murdered also. Earlier, in scene 5, Claudius told Gertrude that his kingship would protect him, forgetting that it did not protect his brother. We may therefore suspect that Claudius is more worried than he reveals and that, as here, he is always quick to act to preserve his own safety, if possible by manipulating others. That Claudius has a cold and calculating side to him is important, because although his character is relatively undeveloped in the play, we have to be able to see him as a substantial opponent for Hamlet if the battle between them is to hold our attention. Shakespeare is therefore achieving several important ends by making Claudius evil, selfish, intelligent and politically adept whilst at the same time giving his character an intriguing degree of ambiguity as regards his motivation and real feelings. Like Hamlet, Claudius cannot retreat from his current situation, but can only struggle to find a way forwards.

Laertes, was your father dear to you?

Claudius begins his manipulation of Laertes, knowing that he is a young man who is prepared to risk everything for revenge, even his salvation, by seeking Hamlet 'To cut his throat i'th' church.' Claudius has reason to fear Laertes,

Revenge

for in scene 5 the messenger reported that 'The rabble call him lord' and cry 'Laertes shall be king.' Although Laertes enters enthusiastically into Claudius' plot to kill Hamlet, he later repents and thereby reveals nobility in his character. Notice how Laertes illustrates his determination to act with the image of killing Hamlet in a church, recalling for the audience Hamlet's sparing of Claudius in similar circumstances and so reminding the audience of the differences between these two 'revenger' characters. Laertes

Hamlet

will 'dare damnation' in his eagerness to act, whilst Hamlet agonises over his conscience, even though he knows that 'conscience does make cowards of us all' (Act 3, scene 1). Paradoxically, Hamlet is now both a revenger and the object of revenge himself, adding with this parallel yet another layer to the play's depiction of humankind's dual nature; part noble/part base.

There is a willow grows askant the brook...

Ophelia

As Laertes and Claudius complete their plotting of Hamlet's death, Gertrude enters to describe the death of Ophelia. Although this serves the dramatic purpose of sharpening even further the determination of Laertes, it also reminds the audience of Ophelia's last speech and the symbolism of flowers in the play. Gertrude's heart-felt, tender and dignified speech also directs the audience's attention to the change of character she has undergone since her son spoke to her so harshly. In Act 5 we see the grave-digger musing on whether Ophelia took her own life, but the evidence here is for an accident when an 'envious sliver' of the tree broke and Ophelia fell into the stream, although she appears to have made no attempt to save herself subsequently.

Self-test (Questions) Act Four

Uncover the plot

Delete some of the alternatives given, to find the correct plot. Beware possible misconceptions and muddles.

Rosencrantz/The Queen/Ophelia tells Claudius/Laertes/Horatio about Hamlet's killing of Polonius. Rosencrantz and Guildenstern go and find the body. Claudius tells some Lords that Ophelia/Laertes/Hamlet is dangerous/ill/mad and must be treated carefully. Hamlet is to be sent to England/Denmark/Norway. The King sends a letter threatening to make war on England/Denmark/Norway unless they imprison/kill/crown Hamlet. A captain in the army of Laertes/Denmark/Fortinbras reveals that they go to fight over an insignificant castle/piece of land/quarrel.

Hamlet vows that from now on he will have only bloody thoughts/loyal friends/
one mission. Ophelia is behaving madly and sings songs about her father/Hamlet/
a dead lover. When Claudius appears she sings about flowers/a seducer/death.
Laertes arrives with a mob and demands vengeance/money/the throne for his
father. Claudius says he is innocent/will pay/will not abdicate. Ophelia sings
about the death of an old man/the King/Hamlet. Claudius says he will secretly
betray/bribe/help Laertes. Horatio gets a message/letter from Hamlet saying that
on his way to England his ship was sunk/set on fire/captured by pirates.
Rosencrantz and Guildenstern have continued to England/been killed/escaped.
Claudius and Horatio/Osric/Laertes plot a fencing match. The tip of one unblunted
sword will be poisoned by Laertes/Claudius and Laertes/Claudius says he will
poison the food/water/wine Hamlet will be given. Horatio/The Queen/A messenger
announces that Ophelia has drowned/committed suicide/died.

Who? What? Why? When? Where? How?
1 For whom does the King call to guard his door?
2 Whose idea is it to have one of the fencing swords 'unbated'?
3 Who comments, with unconscious irony, that when 'sorrows come, they
   come not in single spies,/But in battalions.'?
4 Complete the following phrase and explain why the speaker is both
   hypocritical and ironic: There's such divinity doth hedge a king...
5 What reason does Claudius give for wanting to poison Hamlet's drink during
   the duel?
6 Who is prepared to cut whose throat in the church?
7 What is it about his father's burial that so distresses and puzzles Laertes?
8 What flower can Ophelia not give her brother and why?
9 What caused Ophelia to drown?
10 According to the messenger, who do the rabble call out to be king?

Who said that?
1 There's rosemary, that's for remembrance...
2 Laertes, was your father dear to you?
3 One woe doth tread upon another's heel,/So fast they follow.
4 Revenge should have no bounds.
5 Now, Hamlet, where's Polonius?
6 ...is't possible a young maid's wits/Should be as mortal as an old man's life?
7 ...some craven scruple/Of thinking too precisely on th' event–
8 The Queen his mother / Lives almost by his looks...
9 Take you me for a sponge, my lord?
10 I cannot choose but weep to think they would lay him i'th' cold ground.

Open quotes
Identify the scene; complete the phrase; identify the speaker and the character
being spoken to.
1 Rightly to be great/Is not to stir without great argument,... (complete next
   two lines)
2 He is dead and gone, lady,/He is dead and gone,... (complete next two lines)
3 How all occasions do inform...
4 There is a willow grows askant the brook...
5 You must not think/That we are made of stuff so flat and dull...
6 Nothing but to show you how a king may go a progress through...
7 ...to my shame I see/The imminent death of twenty thousand men/That, ...
   (complete next five lines)
8 There lives within the very flame of love...
9 O, from this time forth...
10 A certain convocation...

Act 5 Scene 1

A grave-digger and his friend (two clowns) discuss whether Ophelia's death was suicide in the light of the coroner's decision to allow her a Christian burial. Hamlet and Horatio enter and the grave-digger turns out a second skull from the grave he is digging. Hamlet considers the death that awaits all people, however powerful. The grave-digger shows Hamlet the skull of Yorick, who was the king's jester over twenty years earlier. Hamlet recalls how he knew the man when he was a boy and reflects upon the inevitability of death. The funeral procession of Ophelia arrives, accompanied by her brother Laertes and by Claudius and Gertrude. The priest makes it clear that Ophelia should have been buried in unsanctified ground, but for the will of Claudius. Hamlet realises whose funeral it is as Laertes jumps in the grave and they fight each other. Hamlet declares his love for Ophelia and then leaves. Claudius promises Laertes that he will get his revenge on Hamlet.

Alas, poor Yorick

The grave-digger scene serves as a contrasting reminder to the audience that

The Fool

outside the plotting and intrigue of the court there exists an ordinary world where the death of people is a natural conclusion to their lives. Additionally, we see here in Hamlet's fond memories of Yorick and his contemplation of the mortality of humankind an implicit acceptance of his own destiny. This mood of serious reflection is emphasised, not diminished, by the fate Hamlet imagines for great rulers and the grave-digger's musings on how long it will be before a corpse rots in the earth. This lightening of the mood is broken by the sudden arrival of Ophelia's funeral procession.

Sweets to the sweet. Farewell

Gertrude scatters flowers upon the grave of Ophelia and grieves that she has

Ophelia

not instead been able to scatter them upon her bridal bed. Laertes says that Ophelia's innocence will encourage violets to grow on her grave – a flower symbolising the faithfulness so lacking in almost all the other characters in the play. Hamlet's wish that Ophelia never be a breeder of sinners has been granted in a way he did not expect.

Gertrude is being used as a 'messenger' character here in order to emphasise the connection between her and Ophelia and not to illuminate a

Gertrude

facet of her own character. This is an interesting reversal, for just as Gertrude here grieves when she anticipated happiness, so at the start of the play Hamlet feels she should have been grieving for her dead husband, not revelling in the 'incestuous sheets' of his brother's bed. Hamlet and Ophelia have in common a murdered father; a soul tormented by love deserted and betrayed at the hands of others; and the promise of great happiness blighted by an early and undeserved death. Ophelia herself has something in common with other young heroines in Shakespeare – like Juliet – in having nobody to turn to in her hour of greatest need. But unlike Juliet, the character of Ophelia can be seen primarily as a vehicle for the actions and emotions of the main male characters: she is used and wronged by Claudius, Polonius and Hamlet.

I lov'd Ophelia. Forty thousand brothers
Could not with all their quantity of love/Make up my sum.

Hamlet declares his love for Ophelia, reversing his comments to her in Act

Sex, Love
and Marriage

3, scene 1: 'I loved you not'. This and his ranting fight in the grave give confusing signals about the state of his mind. Is it his antic disposition, or his true feelings which we see? It may be that Gertrude's supposition is correct and that her son's grief has here spilled into 'mere madness' which will shortly pass. As in other places, Hamlet's pretended madness has so confused the other characters that they are unable to tell what the real state of his mind is, or why he is the way he is. But it is too late for the love between Hamlet and Ophelia to be recovered. The action of the play – whose ending is anticipated here – sees two sons who in revenging their fathers destroy each other; both are tainted with the evil inherent in the original crime and at the end of the play both die forgiving each other.

Act 5 Scene 2

Hamlet tells Horatio how on the voyage to England he secretly opened the sealed message which Rosencrantz and Guildenstern carried and which he discovered contained instructions that he be beheaded. Hamlet exchanged the message for one demanding the execution of Rosencrantz and Guildenstern. The courtier Osric arrives with Claudius' request that Hamlet take part in a fencing match with Laertes, upon which Claudius has wagered that Hamlet will win. After mocking Osric, Hamlet sends him with a message of acceptance. Hamlet tells Horatio that he feels misgivings about the match but that he is now ready to accept whatever fate has in store for him. During the fencing match Hamlet refuses a drink in which Claudius says he has put a pearl, but Gertrude takes the poisoned cup before Claudius can stop her. The sword fight continues with first Hamlet and then Laertes being wounded with the poisoned sword. Gertrude falls but identifies the drink as being poisoned before she dies. Laertes confesses the truth about the plot and Hamlet wounds Claudius with the poisoned sword, then forces him to drink the poisoned wine. Laertes and Hamlet forgive each other and Laertes dies. Horatio attempts to drink the poisoned wine but Hamlet commands him to live so that others may know what has happened. Ambassadors arrive from England to report the deaths of Rosencrantz and Guildenstern. As Fortinbras returns victorious from Poland, Hamlet declares him successor to the throne, then dies. Fortinbras arrives and commands that Hamlet be given a noble burial.

There's a divinity that shapes our ends, Rough-hew them how we will

It is clear that Hamlet has now fully accepted the role which fate has carved out for him and that he is at peace with the moral conflict inherent in committing a second murder to avenge a first.

It is indifferent cold, my lord, indeed

The Fool

Osric is an amusing version of Polonius, sent here as messenger for the coming duel. Notice how Hamlet and Horatio's viewing of Osric as an amusing distraction subtly hints at Hamlet's own changed relationship with the events of the court – he is no longer emotionally embroiled with the action as he was at the start of the play but is now more detached and resigned about the hand which fate has dealt him and the part he must play. However, we should not overlook the dramatic fact that Osric is, however unintentionally, death's messenger.

Not a whit. We defy augury

Order and Disorder

Hamlet's suggestion is that, as in the biblical story, even the smallest event on earth was part of God's will and he must accept his destiny whatever it may be. The Elizabethan philosophy of a hierarchically ordered universe ordained that man's role in the world order was to obey the dictates of his proper position, accepting that an understanding of the will of fate would always be beyond his reach.

Give me your pardon, sir. I have done you wrong...

Appearance and Reality

This speech resurrects the difficult question of Hamlet's state of mind in the play. Hamlet apologises to Laertes and blames his madness for his recent behaviour. The apology seems sincere but if so raises the issue of how genuine Hamlet's madness really is. It is possible, by reference to the text, to support several positions: the view that Hamlet is not mad but feigns it for his own ends; the view that he initially feigns it but later actually goes mad; or that Hamlet shows signs of madness (or signs of being mentally unbalanced) throughout the entire play from time to time. Hamlet himself talks of his own 'antic disposition' after seeing the Ghost, Claudius seems to think Hamlet definitely mad whilst Gertrude put his behaviour down to 'his father's death, and our o'erhasty marriage', whilst Polonius is convinced it is due to unrequited love for his daughter Ophelia.

Set me the stoups of wine upon that table

Appearance and Reality

Claudius is here running his own deadly and 'baited' version of 'The Mousetrap'. The fencing match is a carefully orchestrated show, a pretence of reality which hides beneath its surface a deadly intent. Shakespeare skilfully balances the differing perceptions of the characters on stage, as set against the audience's understanding of what is taking place, to produce a tense series of interchanges and fencing bouts almost devoid of dialogue – except of the most matter-of-fact sort. Notice how Shakespeare skilfully weaves the many plot strands together in this final scene – how Hamlet, characteristically critical of Claudius' associations with drunkenness, will not take a drink in toast; how Gertrude does so in affection for her son (now that their relationship as mother and son is re-established); and how it is providence which arranges the exchange of swords 'in scuffling'.

Sex, Love and Marriage

Exchange forgiveness with me, noble Hamlet

Revenge

As Laertes dies, he and Hamlet forgive each other, both dying in the cause of revenge. Both have been trapped, in different ways, by the inescapable evil involved in righting a wrong.

Now cracks a noble heart

Order and Disorder

Horatio, as the only major character to avoid being tainted by the poison which has spread out from Claudius, is left to announce the reintroduction of order into the state when Fortinbras arrives as heir to the throne. Fortinbras speaks of Hamlet as having fulfilled a soldier's duty to fight and die for honour upon the field of battle, reminding the audience of Hamlet's observation in Act 4, scene 4: 'rightly to be great is not to stir without great argument, but rightly to find quarrel in a straw when honour's at the stake'.

Self-test (Questions) Act Five

Uncover the plot
Delete some of the alternatives given, to find the correct plot. Beware possible misconceptions and muddles.

Hamlet/A grave-digger/Horatio thinks Ophelia's Christian funeral is strange because some say her death was suicide/murder. A grave-digger turns out a weapon/crown/skull from the grave he is digging. The grave-digger shows Hamlet the skull of Osric/Henrick/Yorick, who was the King's jester/adviser/brother. Hamlet recalls how he knew him when he was at university/abroad/a boy. The funeral procession of Ophelia arrives, accompanied by Laertes/Polonius/Horatio and the King and Queen. Laertes/The priest/Gertrude makes it clear that Ophelia would have been buried in unsanctified ground, but the coroner/the King/her father ordered otherwise. Laertes/Horatio/Claudius jumps in the grave with Fortinbras/Reynaldo/Hamlet and they fight. Horatio learns that on the voyage to England Rosencrantz/Guildenstern/Hamlet secretly opened the message from the King which contained secret instructions. The message was exchanged for one demanding the execution of Fortinbras and Reynaldo/Rosencrantz and Guildenstern/Barnardo and Marcellus. Osric/Francisco/Cornelius arrives with the King's request that Hamlet take part in a fencing match with Horatio/Lamord/Laertes. Hamlet says he is now ready to kill Claudius/accept his fate/obey the Ghost. During the fencing match Ophelia/Horatio/Gertrude takes the poisoned cup of drink before Claudius/Hamlet/Fortinbras can stop her. During the sword fight Laertes/Hamlet and then Laertes/Hamlet is wounded with the poisoned sword. Claudius/Laertes confesses the truth about the plot. Laertes/Hamlet wounds Claudius/Horatio with the poisoned sword, then forces him to drink the poisoned wine. Laertes and Claudius/Hamlet forgive each other, then Laertes dies. Horatio/Fortinbras/Cornelius attempts to drink the poisoned wine but Hamlet commands him to live so that others may know what happened. Fortinbras has returned victorious from Poland/Norway/England and is elected/appointed/named as the next king. Fortinbras commands that Claudius/Hamlet/each of the dead be given a noble burial.

Who? What? Why? When? Where? How?
1   Who 'did make love' to what 'employment'?
2   For how long has the grave-digger been employed in his job?
3   Who, at Ophelia's funeral, says they hoped to have seen her married to Hamlet?
4   How could Hamlet alter the message from Claudius to England without it being detectable?
5   How many characters die in Act 5?
6   Why will a tanner's corpse last longer in the ground than another's, and who says so?
7   Which character identifies the wine as having been poisoned?
8   What prize does Claudius offer Hamlet for scoring the first hit in the fencing match?
9   Who was Yorick?
10 Who confesses that in their heart there has been a kind of fighting which would not let them sleep?

Who said that?
1   I lov'd Ophelia.
2   It is the poison'd cup. It is too late.
3   Now cracks a noble heart.
4   The cat will mew, and dog will have his day.
5   This is too heavy. Let me see another.
6   The readiness is all.
7   His purse is empty already, all's golden words are spent.
8   Argal, he that is not guilty of his own death shortens not his own life.
9   The King – the King's to blame.
10 A hit, a very palpable hit.

Open quotes

Identify the scene; complete the phrase; identify the speaker and the character being spoken to.

1 Alas, poor Yorick. I knew him, Horatio,...
2 Why, as a woodcock to mine own springe, Osric.
3 Good night, sweet prince,...
4 Free me so far in your most generous thoughts/That I have shot my arrow...
5 We defy augury.
6 For he was likely, had he been put on, ...
7 If it be now, 'tis not to come; if it be not to come,...
8 Our indiscretion sometimes serves us well...
9 The King, sir, hath laid, sir, that in a dozen passes between yourself and him...
10 There's a divinity that shapes our ends,...

Self-test (Answers) Act One

Uncover the plot

The castle sentinels Barnardo and Francisco witness the ghost of the dead king, which appears at midnight. The new king Claudius has recently married Gertrude, his brother's wife. The new king has sent a message to the King of Norway to ask his help in calming the warlike ambitions of Fortinbras. The King and Queen do not want Hamlet to go back to Wittenberg, where he has been studying, although the son of Polonius is given leave to go back to his studies in France. Laertes warns his sister Ophelia about Hamlet. Polonius lectures his son about how he should behave whilst away. Polonius forbids Ophelia to see Hamlet again. That night on the castle walls the Ghost again appears and beckons for Hamlet to follow it. The Ghost explains how first Claudius seduced the Queen, and then poisoned him whilst he was sleeping. The Ghost commands Hamlet to avenge his murder but tells him not to harm his mother. The Ghost departs and Hamlet makes the others swear to keep the events of the night a secret.

Who? What? Why? When? Where? How?

1   Hamlet, reflecting upon his mother's remarriage within a month of his father's death
2   The drunkenness of the court
3   The funeral bak'd meats
4   To purge away the sins done whilst he was alive
5   Horatio
6   The Ghost wears its beaver (face-guard) up
7   Less than a month
8   Polonius, talking to Ophelia about why she should discount Hamlet's recent vows of love to her
9   Midnight
10 The Ghost speaks for the first time in Act 1, scene 5 and the last thing it says in that Act is 'Swear'

Who said that?

1   Hamlet (I.ii)
2   Hamlet (I.ii)
3   Polonius (I.iii)
4   Hamlet (I.iv)
5   Marcellus (I.iv)
6   The Ghost (I.v)
7   Horatio (I.v)
8   Laertes (I.iii)
9   Hamlet (I.ii)
10 Horatio (I.i)

Open quotes

1   Walks o'er the dew of yon high eastward hill. Horatio, talking to Marcellus and Barnardo in Act 1, scene 1
2   Than is the throne of Denmark to thy father. Claudius, talking to Laertes in Act 1, scene 2
3   ... I have that within which passes show,/These but the trappings and the suits of woe. Hamlet, talking to his mother in Act 1, scene 2
4   and unprofitable/Seem to me all the uses of this world! Hamlet, soliloquy in Act 1, scene 2

5   And it must follow as the night the day/Thou canst not then be false to any man. Polonius, advising his son in Act 1, scene 3

6   May sweep to my revenge. Hamlet, speaking to the Ghost in Act 1, scene 5

7   a celestial bed/And prey on garbage. The Ghost, speaking to Hamlet in Act 1, scene 5

8   That one may smile, and smile, and be a villain. Hamlet, soliloquy in Act 1, scene 5

9   joint. O cursed spite,/That ever I was born to set it right. Hamlet, talking to Horatio and Marcellus at the end of Act 1

Self-test (Answers) Act Two

Uncover the plot

Polonius instructs Reynaldo, who is going to visit Laertes, to spy upon him. Ophelia says that Hamlet has been behaving very strangely. Polonius is convinced that this is because of his love for Ophelia. The King and Queen welcome Hamlet's friends from Wittenberg. Messengers return with news that the Norwegian King now seeks permission for safe passage for his army through Denmark. Polonius produces letters to Ophelia from Hamlet and gets the King and Queen to agree to setting a trap for him. Hamlet says he knows that his friends have been sent to observe him. A travelling group of players arrive and Hamlet welcomes them. The players agree to include some lines by Hamlet to be added into their play for the court. When alone on stage, Hamlet criticises himself for his delay.

Who? What? Why? When? Where? How?

1   Polonius, who loses his train of thought whilst giving advice
2   Rosencrantz and Guildenstern
3   Ophelia's description of Hamlet's appearance to her
4   Out of duty and obedience to her father
5   His job is to secretly observe Laertes
6   His father's recent death and her over-hasty marriage to the King
7   A man
8   The King of Norway gives this money to Fortinbras as a fee for taking his army to attack Poland
9   He has bad dreams
10 Claudius says he thinks this of Polonius

Who said that?

1   Polonius (II.ii)
2   Hamlet (II.ii)
3   Polonius (II.i)
4   Guildenstern (II.ii)
5   Rosencrantz (II.ii)
6   Hamlet (II.ii)
7   Hamlet (II.ii)
8   Polonius (II.ii)
9   Hamlet (II.ii)
10 Ophelia (II.i)

Open quotes

1 By indirections find directions out. Polonius, talking to Reynaldo in Act 2, scene 1
2 but thinking makes it so. Hamlet, talking to Rosencrantz and Guildenstern in Act 2, scene 2
3 lost all my mirth, forgone all custom of exercises... Hamlet, talking to Rosencrantz and Guildenstern in Act 2, scene 2
4 yet there is method in't. Polonius in an aside whilst talking to Hamlet in Act 2, scene 2
5 When the wind is southerly, I know a hawk from a handsaw. Hamlet, talking to Guildenstern in Act 2, scene 2
6 less art. Gertrude, becoming impatient with Polonius in Act 2, scene 2
7 John-a-dreams, unpregnant of my cause,/And can say nothing – no, not for a king. Hamlet, soliloquy at the end of Act 2
8 That I have positively said ''Tis so',/When it prov'd otherwise? Polonius, talking to the King and Queen in Act 2, scene 2
9 Wherein I'll catch the conscience of the King. Hamlet, soliloquy at the end of Act 2
10 how noble in reason, how infinite in faculties, in form and moving how express and admirable, in action how like an angel, in apprehension how like a god: Hamlet, talking to Rosencrantz and Guildenstern in Act 2, scene 2

Self-test (Answers) Act Three

Uncover the plot
The King and Polonius hide to watch a meeting of Hamlet and Ophelia. Hamlet criticises all women for their falseness. Ophelia is convinced that Hamlet has gone mad. The King says he will send Hamlet to England and agrees to let Polonius spy on a meeting between Hamlet and the Queen. Hamlet instructs the players in the art of acting. Hamlet asks Horatio to watch the King's reactions during the play that evening. Claudius leaves the play abruptly and Hamlet is convinced this is evidence of his guilt. Polonius says the Queen wants to see Hamlet but is mocked for his obsequious manner. Hamlet vows not to use physical violence towards his mother as he goes off to see her. Rosencrantz and Guildenstern are told they must go immediately to England. Polonius says he will hide behind the arras to spy on Hamlet's meeting with Gertrude. When the King is alone, he confesses he murdered his brother but says he cannot see how forgiveness can be his. As the King tries to pray Hamlet appears and considers killing him but decides against it because the King might go to heaven. When Hamlet meets his mother she becomes frightened and Polonius cries out; Hamlet kills him by thrusting his rapier through the curtain. Hamlet then criticises his mother for being involved in killing his father and for marrying Claudius. The Ghost appears and Hamlet talks to it. Gertrude is now convinced Hamlet is mad. Hamlet says he is only pretending and makes her promise to keep his secret. Hamlet says he does not trust his school fellows and that he is going away to England.

Who? What? Why? When? Where? How?
1 To his mother, in Act 3, scene 4, to get her to rebuff the King's amorous and sexual advances and not to reveal Hamlet's secret

2   It provokes the conscience of the King into making him reveal (in an aside) his guilt for the first time
3   The 'undiscover'd country' which is death
4   Hamlet says this of all women, when talking to Ophelia in the 'nunnery' scene in Act 3, scene 1
5   When he sees that it is Polonius, he says 'I took thee for thy better', meaning the King
6   Polonius is described as such by Hamlet, speaking to Gertrude immediately after Hamlet has killed him
7   The actors are advised of this by Hamlet, who is concerned that they do not overact their scenes
8   To remind him of his promise to avenge his father's murder, because he has not so far discharged this responsibility
9   Hamlet tells her this because he is feeling disillusioned with humankind and so that she will be safe from falling in love, from getting married and from having children, who will then become sinners and wicked people, like everyone else
10 The fear which surrounds the unknown fate which awaits all mankind after death

Who said that?
1   Hamlet (III.i)
2   Claudius (III.iii)
3   Hamlet (III.iv)
4   Hamlet (III.ii)
5   Claudius (III.iii)
6   Hamlet (III.ii)
7   Claudius (III.i)
8   Gertrude (III.ii)
9   Hamlet (III.iv)
10 Hamlet (III.ii)

Open quotes
1   for a thousand pound. Hamlet, talking to Horatio in Act 3, scene 2
2   The counterfeit presentment of two brothers. Hamlet, talking to his mother about the contrast between his father and Claudius in Act 3, scene 4
3   as I will adders fang'd. Hamlet, talking to the Queen about Rosencrantz and Guildenstern in Act 3, scene 4
4   Whether 'tis nobler in the mind to suffer/The slings and arrows of outrageous fortune,/Or to take arms against a sea of troubles/And by opposing end them. Hamlet, soliloquy in Act 3, scene 1
5   To make them ranker. Hamlet, talking to his mother after the Ghost has departed, in Act 3, scene 4
6   O step between her and her fighting soul./Conceit in weakest bodies strongest works./Speak to her, Hamlet. The Ghost, talking to Hamlet in Act 3, scene 4
7   Hoist with his own petard. Hamlet, talking to the Queen in Act 3, scene 4
8   And there I see such black and grained spots/As will not leave their tinct. The Queen, talking to Hamlet in Act 3, scene 4
9   it smells to heaven;/It hath the primal eldest curse upon't –/A brother's murder. Claudius, soliloquy in Act 3, scene 3

Self-test (Answers) Act Four

Uncover the plot

The Queen tells Claudius about Hamlet's killing of Polonius. Rosencrantz and Guildenstern go and find the body. Claudius tells some Lords that Hamlet is dangerous and must be treated carefully. Hamlet is to be sent to England. The King sends a letter threatening to make war on England unless they kill Hamlet. A captain in the army of Fortinbras reveals that they go to fight over an insignificant piece of land. Hamlet vows that from now on he will have only bloody thoughts. Ophelia is behaving madly and sings songs about a dead lover. When Claudius appears she sings about a seducer. Laertes arrives with a mob and demands vengeance for his father. Claudius says he is innocent. Ophelia sings about the death of an old man. Claudius says he will secretly help Laertes. Horatio gets a letter from Hamlet saying that on his way to England his ship was captured by pirates. Rosencrantz and Guildenstern have continued to England. Claudius and Laertes plot a fencing match. The tip of one unblunted sword will be poisoned by Laertes and Claudius says he will poison the wine Hamlet will be given. The Queen announces that Ophelia has drowned.

Who? What? Why? When? Where? How?

1   His Switzers (royal guards, sometimes spelt Swissers). Swiss mercenaries were often used as royal guards in Europe, underlining that Claudius is well guarded
2   Claudius's
3   Claudius, talking about Ophelia's distressed state in IV.v at the death of her father – ironic because it foreshadows many other deaths to come, including his own
4   That treason can but peep to what it would,/Acts little of his will. Hypocritical because Claudius gained the throne through treason and King Hamlet's 'divinity' was no protection to him; ironic because he will die by his own treason
5   In case the poisoned sword of Laertes for some reason does not work
6   Laertes says – in Act 4, scene 7 – that he is prepared to do this to Hamlet
7   His funeral was 'obscure', with nothing on his grave to mark his noble status and no noble rites to honour him
8   Violets, because they all withered when her father died
9   Her clothes became soaked with water and pulled her under water, after the branch broke and she fell into the brook
10 Laertes

Who said that?

1   Ophelia (IV.v)
2   Claudius (IV.vii)
3   Gertrude (IV.vii)
4   Claudius (IV.vii)
5   Claudius (IV.iii)
6   Laertes (IV.v)
7   Hamlet (IV.iv)
8   Claudius (IV.vii)
9   Rosencrantz (IV.ii)
10 Ophelia (IV.v)

Open quotes

1 But greatly to find quarrel in a straw/When honour's at the stake. Hamlet, soliloquy at the end of Act 4, scene 4

2 At his head a grass-green turf,/At his heels a stone. Ophelia, song in Act 4, scene 5

3 against me,/And spur my dull revenge. Hamlet, soliloquy at the end of Act 4, scene 4

4 That shows his hoary leaves in the glassy stream. The Queen, talking about Ophelia's drowning, in Act 4, scene 7

5 That we can let our beard be shook with danger/And think it pastime. Claudius, talking to Laertes in Act 4, scene 7

6 the guts of a beggar. Hamlet, talking to Claudius in Act 4, scene 3

7 for a fantasy and trick of fame,/Go to their graves like beds, fight for a plot/ Whereon the numbers cannot try the cause,/Which is not tomb enough and continent/To hide the slain? Hamlet, soliloquy at the end of Act 4, scene 4

8 A kind of wick or snuff that will abate it. Claudius, talking to Laertes in Act 4, scene 7

9 My thoughts be bloody or be nothing worth. Hamlet, soliloquy at the end of Act 4, scene 4

10 of politic worms are e'en at him. Hamlet, talking to the King about Polonius in Act 4, scene 3

Self-test (Answers) Act Five

Uncover the plot

A grave-digger thinks Ophelia's Christian funeral is strange because some say her death was suicide. A grave-digger turns out a skull from the grave he is digging. The grave-digger shows Hamlet the skull of Yorick, who was the King's jester. Hamlet recalls how he knew him when he was a boy. The funeral procession of Ophelia arrives, accompanied by Laertes and the King and Queen. The priest makes it clear that Ophelia would have been buried in unsanctified ground, but the King ordered otherwise. Laertes jumps in the grave with Hamlet and they fight. Horatio learns that on the voyage to England Hamlet secretly opened the message from the King which contained secret instructions. The message was exchanged for one demanding the execution of Rosencrantz and Guildenstern. Osric arrives with the King's request that Hamlet take part in a fencing match with Laertes. Hamlet says he is now ready to accept his fate. During the fencing match Gertrude takes the poisoned cup of drink before Claudius can stop her. During the sword fight Hamlet and then Laertes is wounded with the poisoned sword. Laertes confesses the truth about the plot. Hamlet wounds Claudius with the poisoned sword, then forces him to drink the poisoned wine. Laertes and Hamlet forgive each other, then Laertes dies. Horatio attempts to drink the poisoned wine but Hamlet commands him to live so that others may know what happened. Fortinbras has returned victorious from Poland and is named as the next king. Fortinbras commands that Hamlet be given a noble burial.

Who? What? Why? When? Where? How?

1 Rosencrantz and Guildenstern were willing agents (made love) to the task (their employment) given them by Claudius

2 Since the day of Hamlet's birth, thirty years ago
3 Gertrude
4 Because he had with him his father's signet and was able to reseal the altered commission with that
5 Four
6 The grave-digger says this is because his hide is tanned with his trade and will keep out the water
7 Gertrude
8 A pearl
9 He was the King's jester
10 Hamlet, when talking to Horatio at the start of scene 2 in Act 5

Who said that?

1 Hamlet (V.i)
2 Claudius (V.ii)
3 Horatio (V.ii)
4 Hamlet (V.i)
5 Laertes (V.ii)
6 Hamlet (V.ii)
7 Horatio (V.ii)
8 The grave-digger (V.i)
9 Laertes (V.ii)
10 Osric (V.ii)

Open quotes

1 a fellow of infinite jest, of most excellent fancy. Hamlet, talking to Horatio in Act 5, scene 1
2 I am justly kill'd with mine own treachery. Laertes, confessing to having poisoned the rapier with which Hamlet wounds him in Act 5, scene 2
3 And flights of angels sing thee to thy rest. Horatio, speaking over Hamlet's dead body in Act 5, scene 2
4 o'er the house/And hurt my brother. Hamlet, asking forgiveness of Laertes before their fencing match in Act 5, scene 2
5 There is special providence in the fall of a sparrow. Hamlet, talking to Horatio in Act 5, scene 2
6 To have prov'd most royal. Fortinbras, when speaking about Hamlet in Act 5, scene 2
7 it will be now; if it be not now, yet it will come. Hamlet, talking to Horatio about his own fate in Act 5, scene 2
8 When our deep plots do pall. Hamlet, talking to Horatio in Act 5, scene 2
9 he shall not exceed you three hits. Osric, talking to Hamlet in Act 5, scene 2 about the arrangements for the fencing match
10 Rough-hew them how we will. Hamlet, talking to Horatio in Act 5, scene 2